Stratified Nature in Women's Writing

Stratified Nature in Women's Writing:

Past, Present, and Future

Edited by

Marie Hendry

Cambridge Scholars Publishing

Stratified Nature in Women's Writing: Past, Present, and Future

Edited by Marie Hendry

This book first published 2023

Cambridge Scholars Publishing

Lady Stephenson Library, Newcastle upon Tyne, NE6 2PA, UK

British Library Cataloguing in Publication Data
A catalogue record for this book is available from the British Library

ISBN (10): 1-5275-9401-7
ISBN (13): 978-1-5275-9401-2

TABLE OF CONTENTS

ACKNOWLEDGMENTS

I want to express my heartfelt thanks to Jeff Darwin for his artwork and design on the cover and support for this project. I also wish to thank Justin Wlazlo for his help in editing and formatting this volume. Thanks also go to the contributors and Cambridge Scholars Publishing for their work and faith in this collection.

INTRODUCTION

MARIE HENDRY

The many ways humans viscerally interact with the planet's ecosystem can be seen throughout the study of literature. Within literary history is often the discourse between human and nature; however, literature by people who identify as women offers a unique perspective on the ways humans interact with their environment. As Selma Lagerloff, the first woman to win the Nobel Prize in Literature, describes in her first novel, *Gösta Berling's Saga* (1891):

> If the things of the world can love, if earth and water can distinguish between friends and enemies, then I would gladly win their love. I would wish that the earth did not feel my steps to be a heavy burden, and that it forgave that for me it was hurt by plough and harrow, and that it would willingly open its arms to receive me when I die. I would wish that the water, whose shining mirror I break with my oar, had the same patience with me as a mother with an eager child who clambers on her knees without a thought to the silk dress donned for the great occasion. I would be friends with the clear air that trembles over the blue mountains, and with the shining, glittering sun and the beautiful stars, for it often seems to me that dead things feel and suffer with the living—the gulf between us is not so wide as we imagine. What portion of the world is there that has not taken part in life's circle?[1]

As Lagerloff shows, nature and the person are interwoven, as this collection connects the nature and expressions of the self.

Stratified Nature: Rethinking Women's Writing in the Anthropocene is a diverse collection that showcases women's writing from around the globe from different time periods. The collection illustrates the many ways the Anthropocene can be approached while studying women's nature writing. Each essay reflects a different approach to the works and develops a larger concept of the Anthropocene through critical interpretation. In compiling the essays, the major focus was the Anthropocene as a whole, as is seen in

---

[1] Lagerlöf, Selma. *Gösta Berling's Saga.* Edited by Greta Anderson, Iowa City, Iowa. Penfield Press, 1997, 269.

the first chapters by Jim Coby and Teresa Fitzpatrick. Their discussions on the Anthropocene, and the works they focus on, help drive the rest of the collection's ethos where critical interpretations of international pieces and the Anthropocene help develop the concepts in the text. These interpretations range from discussions on Willa Cather's works by Arush Pande and Laura Holder in their respective chapters, to more modern works such as Wendy Whelan-Stewart's approach to breastfeeding in Maggie Nelson's *The Argonauts* (2015) and Hatice Bay's discussion of Imbolo Mbue's 2021 work *How Beautiful We Were*.

Each of the following chapters approaches women's nature writing and the Anthropocene in unique and challenging ways, showing the importance of studying how women-identifying literature approaches the ever-changing concept of the Anthropocene.

CHAPTER ONE

LIFE AFTER DEATH IN LYDIA MILLET'S
A CHILDREN'S BIBLE

JIM COBY

In his provocative 2016 study *The Great Derangement: Climate Change and the Unthinkable*, Amitav Ghosh lamented that he found a relative dearth of fiction addressing climate change when compared to fiction exploring other issues of our time. He writes, "That climate change casts a much smaller shadow with the landscape of literary fiction than it does even in the public arena is not hard to establish."[1] A persuasive starting point, but Ghosh quickly slips into the trappings of championing one genre over another by offering "the mere mention of the subject [of climate change] is often enough to relegate a novel or a short story to the genre of science fiction."[2] Although Ghosh exhausts few resources exploring whether or not he personally believes science fiction a capable vehicle for carrying conversations about climate change, he clearly suggests that the general public and academic readership of such texts relegate science fiction works to a lower rung of fiction, one that need not be taken seriously nor even encountered. Ignoring issues with generic demarcations, what we can intuit from Ghosh's complaint is that more authors need to take seriously, even direly, the increasingly uneasy climate landscape which scientists expect us to encounter. Encouragingly, in the few years since Ghosh published his inchoate argument, a wellspring of popular, literary fiction addressing the topics of climate change and the Anthropocene has emerged. Indeed, Matthew Schneider-Mayerson, an assistant professor of social sciences, recently explained to *The Grist*, "I think we're close to the point where

---

[1] Ghosh, Amitav, *The Great Derangement: Climate Change and the Unthinkable*, (U of Chicago P, 2016), 7
[2] Ghosh, *The Great Derangement: Climate Change and the Unthinkable*, 7

literature that doesn't include climate change, in some way, shape, or form, just isn't reflecting the reality that we inhabit."[3]

But addressing climate change in fiction can be exceptionally challenging. Aside from the concerns that Ghosh raises, the temporality of the subject also presents thorny problems. Climate change rarely provides moments of immediacy. Undoubtedly, we can point to hurricanes of unprecedented strength making landfall far earlier or later than the traditional season; we can observe blizzards affecting even the deepest portions of the American Deep South; we see (and breathe) the now ubiquitous summer wildfires ravaging throughout California, Washington, and Oregon, and whose attendant smoke affects air quality across the continent. But moments like this pale in comparison to the long term, more minute changes that will be experienced only tangentially by those living today but will instead be the inheritance for the generations following our own. The question, then, of how to grapple with a subject as immense and perilous as climate change is one that has plagued scholars in recent years. "What," wonders Adam Trexler, "tropes are necessary to comprehend climate change or to articulate the possible futures faced by humanity? How can a global process, spanning millennia, be made comprehensible to human imagination, with its limited sense of place and time?"[4] As if speaking directly to the complexities inherent to Trexler's inquiries, recent scholarship suggests that not only do we need to wrestle with ideas or narrative, but we perhaps need to reevaluate the very language we use to understand climate change. For example, Timothy Morton seeks to make comprehensible the vast temporalities at the heart of Trexler's second question in his scholarship addressing *hyperobjects*. In *Being Ecological*, Morton defines the concept of a hyperobject as any "entity that is massively distributed in space and time in such a way that you obviously can only access small slices of it *at a time*, and in such a way that obviously transcends merely human access modes and scales" (italics in original).[5] If we're in fact dealing with one of the most remarkable, capacious, affecting, and overwhelming subjects that humankind (or any other *kind* for that matter) has ever confronted, then it makes sense we should engage with equally capacious, overwhelming, and influential texts as a means of helping us to make sense of what existence may feasibly look like in the near and far future. As Morton rightly notes,

---

[3] Yoder, Kate, "With the world on fire, climate fiction no longer looks like fantasy," *The Grist*, (20 Oct. 2020), https://grist.org/climate/with-the-world-on-fire-climate-fiction-no-longer-looks-like-fantasy/.
[4] Trexler, Adam, *Anthropocene Fictions: The Novel in a Time of Climate Change*, (U of Virginia P, 2015), 5
[5] Morton, Timothy, *Being Ecological*, (Pelican, 2018), 125

however, such visions prove elusive, in that we tend to only be able to visualize small parts of the greater whole, and so visualizing the sweeping scope of climate change through fiction becomes a Herculean, but necessary endeavor. Enter Lydia Millet.

In the tumultuous spring of 2020, Lydia Millet, a writer and longtime employee at the Center for Biological Diversity, published her novel, *A Children's Bible* to near unanimous acclaim, with reviewers, such as Ron Charles of *The Washington Post*, championing the work as a "blistering classic," a phrase that, as we shall see shortly, evokes Millet's deep entanglements with antiquity, the contemporary, and futurity. The novel initially concerns a reunion between several middle-aged friends in a rented coastal house in some imagined New England coastal community and its attendant debaucherous, drunken consequences. These escapades all occur under the watchful and sardonic eyes of their disgusted teenage children. Things devolve quickly, however, as a hurricane of unheralded proportions devastates the home and its surrounding environs. In the midst of these environmental collapses, the children emerge as the more capable, caring, and resilient in dealing with the myriad calamities, both environmental and manmade, that descend upon the families. And so, what begins as a satire of fifty-somethings desperately attempting to recapture their youth mutates into "an indictment of a generation's failure to deal with climate change" ("Talking About").[6]

Speaking on the *New York Times' Book Review* Podcast, critic Emily Aiken notes that alongside its more blatant environmental arguments, the novel is "populated with allusions to the Bible [...] cleverly interpolated into the plot." ("Talking About").[7] Once readers begin to notice Millet's patterns and allusions, the novel opens itself to countless re-readings, with each exposing new and ever more complicated references to stories from the Old and New Testaments. Throughout the novel, readers witness a Moses figure floating on a life raft, a bush with flowers so bright they almost look aflame, and three wise hikers who emerge from the Appalachian Trail just in time to witness a birth in a barn, among countless others. While Emily Aiken explores a few of these allusions, she offers no entry point for the allusions' meaning, coyly suggesting, "I'll leave it up to you, Millet's readers, to decide what she's up to here, but she's not a religious writer or an irreligious

---

[6] "Talking About the 10 Best Books of 2020," *The Book Review* (The New York Times, 27 Nov. 2020),
https://www.nytimes.com/2020/11/27/books/review/podcast-10-best-books-2020.html.

[7] "Talking About the 10 Best Books of 2020"

writer."[8] And such is the aim of this paper - to figure out what Millet is "up to," and to explore the allusions - Biblical and otherwise - present in Millet's novel to better grasp how antiquity, the present, and speculative futures combine a compelling and heart-wrenching exploration of familial relations and the inevitability of climate catastrophe.

Over the course of this novel, Millet explores various modes of storytelling and addressing climate change as a way of confronting the overwhelming and, in many ways, the incomprehensibility of such a gargantuan temporality as that in which climate change resides. One of the ways Millet approaches this subject is by having her younger characters critique, often viciously, the in/actions of their parents and other older people that surround them. The novel's narrator, Evie, reveals early on that the children have made a game of distancing themselves from their elders. "Hiding our parentage was a leisurely pursuit," she remarks, "but one we took seriously."[9] Throughout the novel, younger characters perform every action within their power to obfuscate their relationships to the parents, and even develop an awards system to commend those who most successfully hide their lineage, a game that initially reeks of ageism and teenage angst. Evie's comments about parents' dancing as a "sad spectacle" in which "they flopped, blasting their old time music"[10] do little to elicit sympathy toward the children, and, indeed, instinctively garner some degree of pity toward the parents. But Evie's comments are no simple malice; they do not reflect a reactionary and shallow distaste for the adults merely because they are adults. Instead, Evie and her cadre's response to their parents' actions emerge from the younger people's awareness of the imminent dangers of climate change and their parents' unwillingness or ineptitude to attempt to resolve any sort of issue, to do *anything* beyond maintaining a stagnant and obstinate "attitude: business as usual."[11]

An early scene at a nightly dinner, the only event where the older people require that their progeny join them, sharply reveals Evie's, and by extension her peers', attitudes toward the parents' treatments of climate crisis. Millet writes, the parents "sat us down and talked about nothing. They aimed their conversation like a dull gray beam. It hit us and lulled us into a stupor. What they said was so boring it filled us with frustration, and after more minutes, rage."[12] Millet here astutely comments on the narcotic quality of the parents' speech. The conversations, with all of their inanity and

---

[8] "Talking About the 10 Best Books of 2020"
[9] Millet, Lydia, *A Children's Bible*, (Norton, 2020), 5.
[10] Millet, Lydia, *A Children's Bible*, 5.
[11] Millet, Lydia, *A Children's Bible*, 28.
[12] Millet, Lydia, *A Children's Bible*, 4.

pointlessness, engender first a type of soporific or numbing quality; the children, like their parents, find respite in conversations that avoid contentious or incendiary issues. In essence, the parents embody a pernicious and fatal mindset that plagues much of the global population. As Michael A. Smyer writes in *Scientific American*, "We're not in climate change denial; we are in avoidance."[13] Much like the alcohol that dulls the parents' sense of impropriety, refusal to engage in difficult discussions allows the parents to not only believe themselves upstanding global citizens, but also to abscond any sort of individual responsibility. As Evie will later reveal, "The parents insisted on denial as a tactic. Not a science denial exactly - they were liberals. It was more denial of reality."[14] Maintaining the status-quo becomes the modus operandi for the parents, and the bane of existence for the children. Evie's language quickly changes, however, and the anaesthetic banality of the parents' conversation gives rise to a type of righteous fury. The aforementioned rage spills over into Evie furiously questioning, "Didn't they know there were urgent subjects? Questions that needed to be asked?"[15] Evie and her compatriots willingness and desire to engage with more pressing matters leads to a steadfast avoidance from the parents. "If one of us said something serious, they dismissed it," Millet writes.[16] So while parents' corporealities undoubtedly upset the taut, svelte young people, it is more their parents' willful avoidance of seismic, global problems, and their concomitant poverty of imagination in theorizing and proposing solutions to those problems, that so upsets their children. This conflict is further exacerbated by the young people's awareness that they will be the ones to receive the first brunt of the climate crisis, not their parents.

Shortly after the group of young people decide to abandon the summer home in favor of finding a beachfront camping spot for the evening, Evie contemplates that she will be the one responsible for revealing to Jack, her younger brother, that their lives will be appreciably more difficult due to climate change. She explains, "We knew who was responsible, of course: it had been a done deal before we were born."[17] In this comment, Evie reveals an awareness of the reality she will be forced to confront, as well as the temporality of the problem. If, as Morton and Ghosh complained, climate

---

[13] Smyer, Michael A., "How Can We Avoid Climate Avoidance?" *Scientific American*, (7 Sept. 2018), https://blogs.scientificamerican.com/observations/how-can-we-avoid-climate-avoidance/.

[14] Millet, Lydia, *A Children's Bible*, 28.

[15] Millet, Lydia, *A Children's Bible*, 4.

[16] Millet, Lydia, *A Children's Bible*, 4.

[17] Millet, Lydia, *A Children's Bible*, 27.

change becomes difficult to conceptualize because of the sheer scale of the problem, then Millet attempts to ameliorate the issue by having a young character cognizant of the scope of climate change, as well as her transitional position within it - that she will face some of the detriment, but not necessarily the worst of it. In short, Evie is able and willing to conceptualize difficult truths and scenarios that the adults of the novel consciously avoid. And it is this failure of the imaginative capacity that Millet takes aim at throughout the rest of her novel. By consciously stylizing her text in a way that homages other genres and texts, she proposes new ways of understanding our current climate crises, and ways of employing texts of the past to understand the climate of the future. One of the pressing concerns in Millet's text is what sort of ecologies await future generations. Morose on its surface, the concern actually proves quite life-affirming. As Samuel Scheffler proposes, "Although we know that humanity won't exist forever, most of us take it for granted that the human race will survive, at least for a while, after we ourselves are gone."[18] This assumption, Scheffler believes, provides us with a sense of stability and a degree of comfort when considering our own inevitable deaths, because "However self-interested or narcissistic we may be, our capacity to find purpose and value in our lives depends on what we expect to happen to others after our deaths."[19] Which is to say, knowing that we leave behind residues of our existences, ideally through art and the lessons which can be drawn from that art, provides an implicit sense of relief against the tides of horror awaiting one confronting death.

Millet's novel begins auspiciously enough, with the whimsical line "Once we lived in a summer country."[20] That the narrative takes place in a "summer country" strikes readers as endearing and perhaps engenders nostalgia for those never-ending August (and august) days of youth. Millet, however, promptly and deftly undermines any sort of comfort that might be drawn from the locale or time frame. That the fecundity and plenty suggested by the summer accompany the past tense of "lived" highlights nothing so much as the innate bygoneness of the world Millet images and the inability to return to such a place. Furthermore, beginning her sentence and story with the single word "once" evokes the notion that what we will be encountering mirrors the "once upon a time" world of fairy tales. Which

---

[18] Scheffler, Samuel, "The Importance of the Afterlife. Seriously," *Modern Ethics in 77 Arguments: A Stone Reader*, edited by Peter Catapano and Simon Critchley, (Liveright, 2017), 415.

[19] Scheffler, Samuel, "The Importance of the Afterlife. Seriously," *Modern Ethics in 77 Arguments: A Stone Reader*, 417

[20] Millet, Lydia, *A Children's Bible*, 1.

is to say, what initially reads as a lighthearted romp through the pastoral mode is revealed to be a lie. The falsity of the premise, much like the idea that climate change can be reversed with only minor changes to our consumerist lifestyles, signals a type of make-believe and delusional understanding of the world that, seemingly, best suits children. The children populating Millet's novel, however, are anything but naive. Indeed, their understanding of their Anthropogenic existence is far more complex than that of the adults in the novel.

These early indications of Millet's and her characters' environmental consciousnesses and their imaginative renderings and understandings of the world they inhabit provides readers with an essential starting point for understanding this work. Beyond its acknowledgement of the text and its setting as inherently a work of artifice, it as well signals the types of fairy tales, mythologies, and oral traditions which lay the bricks of the novel's foundation. Which is to say, Millet very knowingly positions her novel as a modern retelling of tropes from earlier environmental texts as a means of at once addressing environmental concerns that are immediate and new, while appreciating that threat and fear undergird the motivation for countless texts of moral instruction and suasion. A second example of this engagement occurs more obliquely, but nonetheless significantly when her young characters meet a group of wealthy teens camping on the same beach. Irritated by their parents' escapades, the children sail out to a local sandbar to camp for a few days when Evie notices "unwelcome colonists … beached upon our shores."[21] The group witnesses as several teens, walking "billdboard[s] for Abercrombie and Fitch,"[22] invade their privacy leaving their "situation rankled."[23] Evie notices too that their seemingly bucolic scene becomes marred by the falsities represented by the teens: "a majestic yacht in cream and gold"[24] brings them to shore, as opposed to the more retrograde canoes used by Evie's group, and "even their marshmallow sticks were manufactured - we saw them holding metal skewers over a fire."[25] Given Evie and her cohort's environmental awareness and concern, she begins to wonder if the teens somehow remain oblivious to their impending struggle, but this concern becomes moot when Evie hears the teens discuss the various compounds and fallout shelters their parents have secured for the upcoming climate crisis. In short, Evie acknowledges "the parents were

---

[21] Millet, Lydia, *A Children's Bible*, 24.
[22] Millet, Lydia, *A Children's Bible*, 26.
[23] Millet, Lydia, *A Children's Bible*, 25.
[24] Millet, Lydia, *A Children's Bible*, 23.
[25] Millet, Lydia, *A Children's Bible*, 26.

their insurance policy."[26] Through this scene, Millet critiques the false notion that money will help secure a future free from the effects of climate change. The wealthy teens, essentially more economically nimble versions of the novel's heroes, represent the mindset that money wealth will insulate them from the fallout which will leave so much of the human world destitute and bordering on extinction. But finances, of course, are insufficient for securing a livable future devoid of chaos and strife in a time of ecological devastation; no carbon tax will mitigate the damage already set in motion. And as Timothy Morton reminds us in *The Ecological Thought*, "Ecology is profoundly about coexistence. Existence is always coexistence. No man is an island."[27] What the rich teens and their parents fail to realize is their concatenation with every entity - living and non-living - that they encounter and how those entanglements affect both them and others. Millet positions the yachters as foils to the young group's more nuanced version of ecological awareness, but in the scene that follows the two groups' encounter, Millet challenges us to confront the way we dismiss and reject those with whom fundamentally disagree on environmental principles.

After returning from the camping expedition, Evie encounters one of her friends, David, "who'd been notably absent" from the excitement of the afternoon, "sitting on the floor in the corner. With a bottle beside him."[28] Evie chides David for drinking after having consumed so much alcohol at the yacht the previous evening, only to learn that David "stayed sober. Thought [he'd] have to monkey-wrench."[29] Millet here introduces yet another entanglement with an earlier form of environmental protection and activism, another means of grappling with ecological instability: that of eco-terrorism. Laurence Buell explains that "'ecoterrorism' and its cognates form a cluster of related neologisms … coined it would seem almost simultaneously from the right - in order to stigmatize radical activists."[30] Although the label itself reeks of politicization and attempts to categorize activists involved in "carefully targeted sabotage"[31] as reckless and overly violent, the neologism has stuck and has been used to classify the actions of characters in numerous pieces of environmental literature, most significantly in Edward Abbey's *The Monkey Wrench Gang*. While there are certainly still instances of eco-sabotage, the terms, ideas, and actions behind them have largely fallen to the wayside following their cultural apex in the 1990s.

---

[26] Millet, Lydia, *A Children's Bible*, 32.
[27] Morton, Timothy, *Being Ecological*, (Pelican, 2018), 4.
[28] Millet, Lydia, *A Children's Bible*, 55.
[29] Millet, Lydia, *A Children's Bible*, 55.
[30] Millet, Lydia, *A Children's Bible*, 156.
[31] Millet, Lydia, *A Children's Bible*, 157.

As such, to participate in eco-sabotage is to engage with a form of environmental activism that is somewhat antiquated. And for the young character, David, who installs a virus on the yacht's navigation system, the employment of this method proves morally destructive. "Those yacht parents are the worst," David admonishes, "*Those* are the people who ate the planet."[32] Ultimately, David regrets his actions and participation in an ostensibly ecoterorristic plot. Like many of the critics of eco-sabotage and ecoterrorism, David himself in his engagement with "anti-humanistic paradigms of environmental value,"[33] namely that the planet would operate more healthily in the absence of the wealthy yacht-sailing sea-farers. Indeed, of his potential actions, he explains, "I was thinking of a puncture in the fuel tank first. But you know. Gas in the ocean, killing fish. I didn't want to sink to their level. So, I just coded a little virus into the nav system." [34] Ostensibly, David's actions prevent any significant environmental damage because his targeted system doesn't directly engage with natural environs. But David miscalculates. He neglects Barry Commoner's first law of ecology: "everything is related to everything else,"[35] and that serving as the catalyst for the yachters' deaths, while potentially providing a brief moment of schadenfreude, would finally prove to be a pyrrhic victory, in that at only at the expense of David's moral bearings does he find pleasure in eliminating the wealthy sea-farers. In his admonishment of his own actions, David becomes aware that eco-terrorist plots only serve limited good; eco-sabotage may eliminate one minor threat, but that the sweep of climate change is too great, the actions already in motion, and the cards are stacked against him. While eco-terrorism served for Edward Abbey in the mid-twentieth century, the tactics employed by the fictional Monkey Wrench Gang fail Evie and her cohort because they provide only temporary solutions, no long-term plan. As such, it becomes clear that the best course of action is not to attempt to counter the forthcoming environmental tumult, but rather to locate new forms of coexistence with an increasingly trepidatious landscape, and that the way to look forward will be to focus on a text of antiquity, and to engage the lessons taught from generations and civilizations that have undergone their own seismic changes. As Roy Scranton argues, "We must inculcate ruminative frequencies in the human animal by teaching slowness, attention to detail, argumentative rigor, careful reading, and meditative reflection. We must keep our communion

---

[32] Millet, Lydia, *A Children's Bible*, 54.
[33] Buell, Laurence, "What is Called Ecoterrorism," *Gramma: Journal of Theory and Criticism*, (no. 16, vol. 1, 2008), 163.
[34] Millet, Lydia, *A Children's Bible*, 54.
[35] Millet, Lydia, *A Children's Bible*, 29.

with the dead, for they are us, as we are the dead of future generations."[36] The most notable of the ur-texts with which Millet engages is, as the title of her work makes obvious, the Holy Bible. By populating her novel with allusion and explicit references to stories and scenes from the Bible, Millet performs an act which both is and isn't parochial. She first answers Scranton's call by allowing her characters to engage with texts of antiquity as a means of understanding and responding to climate crisis. Beyond that, she includes allusions to a wide array of Biblical narratives from both the Old and New Testaments. As a result, she is able to present a sweeping account of climate change, and one that escapes the trappings of a myopic rendering of climate crisis as a singular event; in essence, she manages to encapsulate the entirety of the hyperobject.

To understand precisely what is at stake in Millet's rendering of the gospel according to climate change, we should first note the sands upon which we foolish men built our homes. We exist now in a geological epoch described as the Anthropocene. This descriptor was first introduced by Paul Crutzen in 2000 to describe "the massive impact by the human species, from the industrial era onward, on our planet's life systems, an impact that, as his term suggests, is geomorphic, equal in force and in long-term implications to a major geological event."[37] If the prospect of humankind's industrial detritus is causing a, quite literal, seismic shift in how various ecologies and environs respond to humankind, we're only making the problem worse. Indeed, some theorists refuse to place such an early entry point (the industrial revolution) to the Anthropocene because recent years have only seen our impacts become exponentially more deleterious. For the characters in Millet's novels, siblings Evie and Jack specifically, the Bible provides a catalyst for understanding and taking charge against the paralytic fear which climate crisis might engender. Early in the novel, an anonymous parent gives Jack, Evie's younger brother and a child with a preternatural gift for textual exegesis, a book entitled *A Child's Bible: Stories from the Old and New Testaments*. The gift strikes Evie as odd given that "for [their] parents religious education wasn't a priority."[38] Nevertheless, Jack immediately begins reading and projecting his own life onto the text. Recounting his reading, Jack explains that the Creation Story "had a talking snake and a lady who really liked fruit."[39] Significantly, he bridges the worlds between

---

[36] Scranton, Roy, *Learning to Die in the Anthropocene: Reflections On the End of a Civilization*, (City Lights Books, 2015), 109.
[37] Nixon, Rob, *Slow Violence and the Environmentalism of the Poor*, (Harvard UP, 2011), 12.
[38] Millet, Lydia, *A Children's Bible*, 43.
[39] Millet, Lydia, *A Children's Bible*, 44.

the text and his own. As Evie notes, the female protagonist "had my name!"[40] In connecting the two worlds, Jack highlights the maneuver for which Scranton so fiercely advocates, finding means of understanding change and climate crisis through examination and rumination on how characters in texts of antiquity have confronted those challenges. Millet further emphasizes this idea when, asked what Jack ultimately believes the story of Adam and Eve to *mean*, he explains, "If you have a nice garden to live in, then you should never leave it."[41] With this, Jack, the novel's youngest character, issues an epiphany evincing a degree of incontrovertible rationality so far beyond the parents' capacity for understanding that he quickly reveals himself to be some degree of prophet, and his interpretations of the Bible become the foundations for understandings of how the young people should react to the various climate crises that emerge.

Allusions to the Bible serve not as a moralizing center, but rather as bedrock for understanding the use of narrative to make sense of traumatic changes. In an attempt to highlight the range of forthcoming climate catastrophes, Millet populates her book with floods, hurricanes, heatwaves, plagues, forced migration, and all other manner of environmental and human threats. Throughout all of it, Jack remains enamored with extrapolating meaning from his Bible. As wind batters the vacation home and a torrential downpour causes banks to overflow and a "toxic soup"[42] of gasoline, pesticides, and various detritus to emerge in the yard, Jack and his companion, Shel, evince agitation and worry, with Jack eventually pleading, "We have to save the animals. Like Noah did."[43] The pair eventually make their camp on a platform in a tree roughly covered by a tarp where they house their menagerie: "There were two doves, a robin, and a small brown bird in a homemade-looking mesh deal. There was a murky terrarium Jack said held crayfish, toads, and a salamander. There were plastic food containers with holes poked in the top, full of silty water and minnows, and a big, fat fish in a cooking pot."[44] As more and more of their ilk flee from their parents' debauchery in the house, the platform earns the name of "Ark."[45] In Millet's most blatant appropriation of Biblical narrative, the story of Noah and the Ark allows Jack to find a sense of purpose and meaning during the midst of an otherwise paralyzing event. Moreover, his actions genuinely benefit others in his immediate orbit: he saves aquatic

[40] Millet, Lydia, *A Children's Bible*, 44.
[41] Millet, Lydia, *A Children's Bible*, 44.
[42] Millet, Lydia, *A Children's Bible*, 72.
[43] Millet, Lydia, *A Children's Bible*, 70.
[44] Millet, Lydia, *A Children's Bible*, 73.
[45] Millet, Lydia, *A Children's Bible*, 77.

creatures from toxic sludge, provides shelter from hail to the birds, and creates a den of respite and safety for all of the other children displaced from the vacation home. In short, Jack applies the principal actions of the Bible story, providing safety to others, free from dogmatism or fundamentalist interpretation. He understands and enacts the story at its most base level, thereby highlighting the utility of engaging with the text during a time of duress.

Aside from embodying Christian typology, Jack also draws meaning from the idea of a Holy Trinity. As Jack notes midway through the novel, "They say God in the book," but "God's a code word … They say God but they mean *nature*."[46] Upon receiving pushback from his peers, Jack wryly replies, "It's a story … Things are *symbols*."[47] Jack's ability to reason both the literal instructions for a type of upright survivalism, as well as his understanding that he's engaging with a deeply metaphorical text underscore precisely the usefulness of such a text - that it serves both a pragmatic and metaphysical purpose. As humanity enters increasingly turbulent and uncertain times, an ability to think critically, creatively, and capaciously will undoubtedly prove a necessity. At the novel's conclusion, his sister Evie explains, "I think you solved it, Jack. [...] Jesus was science. Knowing stuff. Right? And the Holy Ghost was all the things that people make. [...] So maybe art is the Holy Ghost."[48] Which is to say, artistic pursuits become an integral component of grappling with trauma and tumult.

In his treatise on art and climate collapse, *Learning to Die in the Anthropocene*, Roy Scranton declares, "In order to adapt to this strange new world, we're going to need more than scientific reports and military policy. We're going to need new ideas. We're going to need new myths and new stories."[49] Most significant in his argument is the call for new "myths," as he believes that to make sense of inevitable environmental devastation, we must look to texts that have stood the test of time (he particularly champions *The Epic of Gilgamesh*) as a conduit to produce art which addresses the eternal subjects of survival and death. "We must suspend our attachment to the continual press of the present," he argues, "by keeping alive the past, cultivating the info-garden of the archives, reading, interpreting, sorting, nurturing, and, most important, reworking our stock of remembrance."[50]

---

[46] Millet, Lydia, *A Children's Bible*, 87.
[47] Millet, Lydia, *A Children's Bible*, 87.
[48] Millet, Lydia, *A Children's Bible*, 224.
[49] Scranton, Roy, *Learning to Die in the Anthropocene: Reflections on the End of a Civilization*, 19.
[50] Scranton, Roy, *Learning to Die in the Anthropocene: Reflections On the End of a Civilization*, 108.

Scranton believes that humankind can take solace in knowing that *something* will continue beyond their own understanding of time, and the proof we have of this is literatures of antiquity addressing traumas and helping us situate our current existence within those archetypal stories. Millet herself, then, engages with this practice in consciously situating Biblical parallels and allusions within her own narrative.

The Bible, and its parallel narratives to Millet's, serves as a way of grappling with past traumas and finding some degree of comfort by knowing that a future will exist. As Scranton encourages readers to find instruction and comfort in works of antiquity, so too does Millet. With the Bible serving as a type of ur-text, she spins a narrative that engages with both the broader brush strokes of Biblical narrative, while also modernizing the tales to frame them within the context of climate change. The core tenet of the Bible, redemption vis a vis Christ's death and resurrection, becomes less about immortal life, but more about the promise of life after death proposed by Samuel Scheffler earlier in this essay. Through the novel's continued emphasis on the sins and illnesses of the parents parallels the focus on the children, who become a simulacrum for exploring how newer generations grapple with the ecological sins of older generations. Scranton echoes this sentiment, writing,

> Humanity can survive the demise of fossil-fuel civilization and it can survive whatever despotism or barbarism will arise in its ruins. We may even be able to survive in a greenhouse world. … If being human is to mean anything at all in the Anthropocene, if we are going to refuse to let ourselves sink into the futility of life without memory, then we must not lose our few thousand years of hard-won knowledge, accumulated at great cost and against great odds. We must not abandon the memory of the dead.[51]

Millet's engagement with Biblical allusions unearths the memory of the dead for which Scranton so furiously argues. The lessons taught within the Bible remind us of the countless civilizations that have arisen and fallen before us. They remind us of the innumerable apocalypses that preceded our own. And they remind us that throughout humankind has remained. To be sure, such a conceit is not an optimistic one - civilization as we understand it cannot and will not continue. Sustainability is a misnomer; there is no "sustaining" humankind's rapacious lust for resources and its refusal to acknowledge its ever-growing damage to the planet. Nonetheless, something, some*one* will continue to exist, but existence will be hard and guides, be

---

[51] Scranton, Roy, *Learning to Die in the Anthropocene: Reflections On the End of a Civilization*, 108-109.

they geographical or spiritual, will be needed. Millet, through her marriage of the Bible and a contemporary climate novel, creates a parable that provides a light for seeing through darkness ahead.

Simon Estok writes that, "reflecting an increasing public awareness of radical weather events, an increasing degradation of ecosystems, and an accelerated mining of the Earth's non-renewable resources, 'Climate Change Fiction' [...] has flourished."[52] And yet, Estok worries that literary interest does not equate to actionable events. "How is it possible," he wonders, "that both increased awareness among lay people and radical exposure of environmental issues in media can be presented at the very moment in history when there are what seem to be exponential increases in assaults on the environment?"[53] About midway through the novel, Evie questions Jack about his seeming obsession with the Bible. As he pores over its pages, Evie questions him, "What are you doing?" To which he responds, "Decoding."[54] As Scranton suggests might be the case, Jack here locates a sense of comfort in his study of texts of antiquity and in finding stories within the pages of his children's Bible applicable to his own plight. Significantly, through his prolific exegesis, he also locates a significant theme in contemporary environmental study - the necessity of art as a means of contending with and forcing understanding of the effects of climate change. Gayle Clemans explains that creative endeavors are crucial in grappling with climate change because "art can reach us emotionally, intellectually and even physiologically. Highly personal, sensory experiences with art can serve as portals into abstract or difficult topics."[55] In this novel, Millet performs the difficult work of creating a visceral piece of art with tangible and heart-wrenching examples of both the physical and psychological toil of failure to appreciably prepare for climate change. As the children in the novel find solace in their interpretations and reenactments of Biblical scenes, engagements with modes of eco-confrontation, and a dismemberment of pastoral and fairytale tropes, Millet provides lenses through which readers might potentially imagine a future beyond imagining. That is, the characters in the novel present readers with ways in which texts and artistic pursuits can help us think through uncertainty with creativity.

---

[52] Estok, Simon C., "Ecomedia and Ecophobia," *Neohelicon*, (vol. 43, issue 1, 2016), 129.
[53] Estok, Simon C., "Ecomedia and Ecophobia," 129.
[54] Millet, Lydia, *A Children's Bible*, 120.
[55] Clemans, Gayle, "Can Art Help Fight Climate Change? These 4 Seattle-Area Artists Think So," The Seattle Times, (18 Sept. 2019), https://www.seattletimes.com/entertainment/visual-arts/can-art-make-a-difference-in-the-fight-against-climate-change-these-4-seattle-area-artists-think-so/.

Terry Eagleton recently insisted, "By reminding us of our mortality, [literature] can foster in us the virtue of humility. This is a precious accomplishment, since much of our moral trouble springs from the unconscious assumption that we will live forever."[56] And this is precisely the charge which Millet accepts with *A Children's Bible*. In highlighting the intertextuality between her own work and others, specifically the Holy Bible, Millet reifies the ways in which literature can help us understand and make sense of climate catastrophe, how we can remain our most human in inhuman circumstances, and how humanity might live forever.

Bibliography

Buell, Laurence, "What is Called Ecoterrorism," *Gramma: Journal of Theory and Criticism*, (no. 16, vol. 1, 2008), pp. 153-166.

Charles, Ron, "Lydia Millet's 'A Children's Bible' is a Blistering Classic," *The Washington Post*, 12 May 2020, https://www.washingtonpost.com/entertainment/books/lydia-millets-a-childrens-bible-is-a-blistering-classic/2020/05/12/542d4e54-93f2-11ea-91d7-cf4423d47683_story.html.

Clemans, Gayle, "Can Art Help Fight Climate Change? These 4 Seattle-Area Artists Think So," *The Seattle Times*, (18 Sept. 2019), https://www.seattletimes.com/entertainment/visual-arts/can-art-make-a-difference-in-the-fight-against-climate-change-these-4-seattle-area-artists-think-so/.

Commoner, Barry, *The Closing Circle: Nature, Man, & Technology*, (Random House, 1971).

Eagleton, Terry, *How to Read Literature*, (Yale UP, 2013).

Estok, Simon C., "Ecomedia and Ecophobia," *Neohelicon*, (vol. 43, iss. 1, 2016), pp. 127-145.

Ghosh, Amitav, *The Great Derangement: Climate Change and the Unthinkable*, (U of Chicago P, 2016).

Millet, Lydia, *A Children's Bible*, (Norton, 2020).

Morton, Timothy, *Being Ecological*, (Pelican, 2018).

—. *The Ecological Thought*, (Harvard UP, 2010).

Nixon, Rob, *Slow Violence and the Environmentalism of the Poor*, (Harvard UP, 2011).

Scheffler, Samuel, "The Importance of the Afterlife. Seriously," *Modern Ethics in 77 Arguments: A Stone Reader*, edited by Peter Catapano and Simon Critchley, (Liveright, 2017), 415-418.

---

[56] Eagleton, Terry, *How to Read Literature*, (Yale UP, 2013), 48.

Scranton, Roy, *Learning to Die in the Anthropocene: Reflections on the End of a Civilization*, (City Lights Books, 2015).

Smyer, Michael A., "How Can We Avoid Climate Avoidance?" *Scientific American*, (7 Sept. 2018), https://blogs.scientificamerican.com/observations/how-can-we-avoid-climate-avoidance/.

"Talking About the 10 Best Books of 2020," *The Book Review* (The New York Times, 27 Nov. 2020), https://www.nytimes.com/2020/11/27/books/review/podcast-10-best-books-2020.html.

Trexler, Adam, *Anthropocene Fictions: The Novel in a Time of Climate Change*, (U of Virginia P, 2015).

Yoder, Kate, "With the world on fire, climate fiction no longer looks like fantasy," *The Grist*, (20 Oct. 2020), https://grist.org/climate/with-the-world-on-fire-climate-fiction-no-longer-looks-like-fantasy/.

CHAPTER TWO

WISTERIA:
A FEMALE ECOGOTHIC METAPHOR IN
AMERICAN FICTION THROUGH THE AGES

TERESA FITZPATRICK

Women and nature have been intrinsically linked in Western culture, literature, and the Anglo-American popular imagination, "each denigrated with reference to the other" from pastoral, through Romanticism to contemporary fiction, with both "gender" and "nature" presented in literature as social constructs reflecting patriarchal concepts of what they *should* be like.[1] Although feminist theory has attempted to separate the gendered dualist constructs of woman/nature, female corporeality continues to be "strongly associated with nature in Western thought."[2] In nineteenth-century English and French literature, the garden is conceived as a domestic space wherein female gender roles are pedagogically formed within a patriarchal construct.[3] Victorians perceived the garden as an extension of the house, providing an arena for younger females to develop nurturing skills using flowers and plants as surrogate children, redolent of their gender roles as housewife and mother. Moreover, the literary Victorian garden was often depicted as a "coming-of-age" training ground where appropriate adult relationships between genders were forged.[4] Alongside the house, then, the garden has inevitably been designated a female domestic space

---

[1] Greg Garrard, *Ecocriticism* (Oxon: Routledge, 2004), 26.

[2] Stacy Alaimo, *Bodily Natures: Science, Environment and the Material Self* (Bloomington and Indianapolis: Indiana University Press, 2010), 5.

[3] Celine Grasser, "Good Girls versus Blooming Maidens: The Building of Female Middle- and Upper-Class Identities in the Garden, England and France, 1820-1870", in *Secret Gardens, Satanic Mills: Placing Girls in European History, 1750-1960*, edited by Mary Jo Maynes, Birgitte Soland & Christina Benninghaus (Bloomington: Indiana University Press, 2005), 131-146.

[4] Grasser, "Good Girls versus Blooming Maidens", 131-146.

within which patriarchal constructs of both gender and nature are depicted as orderly, controlled, and passive.

"In Victorian imaginative literature, women are frequently presented in the company of flowers," Michael Waters notes, "to heighten their femininity."[5] However, as Female Gothic theories have demonstrated, "Victorian representations of women tend to polar extremes," rendering females as symbols of either "domestic happiness or unnatural monsters."[6] Transgressive women were often associated with monstrous nature. Those women who failed to conform to patriarchal constructs were aligned with wild and uncontrollable nature, while colonial encounters with indigenous females were often described as exotic jungle flowers. This dichotomous perspective of idealised/vilified woman and cultivated/wild nature in the male imagination persists well into the twentieth century, conflating female corporeality and monstrous nature in Gothic texts, and where illicit sexual interactions take place within the formalised garden setting as a way of highlighting female transgressions. Linked with the home, "[t]he very demarcation of green space as enclosed and duly ordered garden," William Hughes explains, "bespeaks a restrictive domestication,"[7] which seen through a Gothic lens, denotes house and garden as a confining female space. One of the frequent visual markers of the confining boundaries of female spaces in fiction is the wisteria – a plant that covers doorways, house fronts and porches. Yet, despite extensive criticism on nature and femininity, there is little research available on the literary significance of wisteria as a gendered metaphor. Using Charlotte Perkins Gilman's ghost story, "The Giant Wistaria" (1891) and Donna A. Leahey's eco-horror story, "The Wisteria" (2014), this paper demonstrates the persistent use of wisteria as an ecogothic metaphor, not just as an indicator of the female domestic space but one that is consistently often a challenging signifier of domestic abuse in Anglo-American fiction and a metaphor that women writers use to haunt the male imagination.

---

[5] Michael Waters, *The Garden in Victorian Literature* (Aldershot: Scholar Press, 1988), 135.
[6] Kelly Hurley, *The Gothic Body* (Cambridge: Cambridge University Press, 1996), 121.
[7] William Hughes, 'Foreword: On the Gothic nature of gardens', in *EcoGothic Gardens in the Long Nineteenth Century: Phantoms, Fantasy and Uncanny Flowers*, edited by Sue Edney (Manchester: Manchester University Press, 2020), xiv-xvii.

Wisteria

A popular climbing plant, with a profusion of pale purple, clustered blossoms that resemble bunches of grapes, this familiar vine was introduced into Western gardens from East Asia during the nineteenth century – an era when exotic plant acquisition provided an indicator of wealth – as a decorative ornamental for porches and trellises. Although young plants often appear quite delicate and require support if they are to be admired in full bloom, established and mature wisteria vines harden and eventually destroy supporting structures.[8] Hardly surprising then, that wisteria has often been associated with patriarchal anxieties about the impact of female independence and with feminist writing. The sinuous vines of plants like wisteria are often equated with transgressive female figures in Judeo-Christian patriarchal culture of the West, evoking images of Eden and Eve's transgression at the behest of the snake in the Tree. Moreover, the wisteria's amazing floral displays and strangling growth offer an ambiguity that reflects the dichotomous attitudes to women within Western cultural tradition. The plant's transgressive imagery is further enhanced by its poisonous seed and anti-clockwise growth that equate it in the male imagination with the *femme fatale* - a Gothic figure that allows for a gendered reading. The trope of the *femme fatale* emerges, according to Rebecca Stott, "from a phallocentric point of view" as the dark, chaotic, irrational, wild side of femininity.[9] French for "deadly woman," the *femme fatale* has long been a figure in literature of wicked seductress and sexual enchantress, who narcissistically manipulates the men around her for her own rewards; a monstrous Other within the dichotomous perspective of idealised/vilified woman in the male imagination. This image of woman as bacchante was used by men "to justify restricting women's rights even further" while women writers employed the *femme fatale* character as a revolutionary figure to serve their own interests "as liberation from the constraints of domesticity."[10] It is my argument that wisteria, both beautiful but poisonous, is associated with this "predatory female" who is often presented as "alluring and deadly,"[11] pointing towards the *femme fatale* figure that "has been used to criticize powerful women" persistently

---

[8] Royal Horticultural Society website: https://www.rhs.org.uk/search?query=wisteria.
[9] Rebecca Stott, *The Fabrication of the Late-Victorian Femme Fatale: The Kiss of Death* (Basingstoke and London: MacMillan Press Ltd, 1992), 38.
[10] Adriana Craciun, *Fatal Women of Romanticism* (Cambridge: Cambridge University Press, 2009), 41.
[11] Stott, *The Fabrication of the Late-Victorian Femme Fatale,* 49.

throughout history, "haunt[ing] Western imagination, materializing whenever male authority feels threatened by female agency."[12] Furthermore, in the hands of female writers, the wisteria demonstrates a vegetal agency that challenges and responds to male violence in the face of female independence.

Encompassing such contradictory attributes offers the wisteria as a plant metaphor within fiction that suggests non-conforming female characters within the phallocentric imagination. In Robert M. Coates's psychological crime thriller, *Wisteria Cottage* (1948), for example, Coates's protagonist, having insinuated himself into the company of a mother and her daughters, becomes increasingly unstable after he accompanies them to a seaside holiday cottage, and they do not adhere to his intended plans. Their eventual brutal murders by the protagonist in response to what he perceives as their transgressions, is subtly indicated, I suggest, in the novel's title through the reference to wisteria. Similarly, Marc Cherry's fictional setting for his 2004-2012 mystery-drama television series, *Desperate Housewives*, is "Wisteria Lane," with the plant reference here again indicative of the transgressions of the idealised suburban female figure, as the suicide/murder of one of their female neighbours sparks the uncovering of domestic abuse, adultery, homicide, and cover-ups in the families along the street. This dark reality hidden behind the façade of suburban perfection, with the manicured lawns and white-picket fences is what Bernice M. Murphy refers to as the Suburban Gothic – a liminal space that is neither city nor rural and epitomizes the 1950s conflict with American conformist ideals.[13] For Murphy, Wisteria Lane depicts "the suburban locale as a place of quiet desperation and festering secrets which, once revealed, are rapidly replaced by yet more darkly enthralling secrets" that must be also be concealed.[14] The wisteria's ambiguous nature – at once impressively floral but highly destructive – positions this plant as a gothic metaphor for women who do not conform to patriarchal expectations and signals the (often violent) oppression such independent behaviour invites within a patriarchal context.

Female writers employ the wisteria's contradictory attributes as a feminist champion for escape from patriarchal domesticity, oppression, and abuse. India Holton, for example, draws on the wisteria's *femme fatale* imagery in her fantasy-romance, *Dangerous Damsels* series, *The Wisteria*

---

[12] Elizabeth Johnston, 'The Original 'Nasty Woman'', *The Atlantic*, 6 November 2016 [accessed: 12 January 2021].
[13] Bernice M. Murphy, *The Suburban Gothic in American Popular Culture* (Basingstoke: Palgrave Macmillan, 2009).
[14] Murphy, *The Suburban Gothic in American Popular Culture*, 168.

Society of Lady Scoundrels (2021).[15] Her story of beautiful female criminals (pirates) in a fantasy Victorian England undermine patriarchal expectations of female behaviour with their demonstrable independence and villainy. What is often vilified in the phallocentric imagination are presented as more positive, with the plant's hardiness, increase in strength and ability to discard controlling support at its moment of full bloom (wisteria only flowers once it has matured), offering wisteria as an ecological metaphor in gothic texts by women writers that signals release from subjugation and the pathway to independence. Given its close association with the house and domestic settings, the wisteria "becomes a complex metaphor for the oppression of women," frequently appearing in gothic tales of female entrapment and patriarchal control.

Porches: wisteria and female space

Being neither inside nor outside, porches occupy an ambiguous relation to the female domestic space. As an add-on area attached to the house, the porch can be seen as bridging the gap between house and garden - a border zone of culture and nature, even more so within an American suburban context where the porch often refers to the elevated covered decking along the outside walls. This is typically where the wisteria is found, adorning porches, decking and doorways; an impressive climber that indicates the boundary of the domestic space. In her essay exploring the American porch as a gendered spatial metaphor, Sue Bidwell Beckham argues the porch was "betwixt and between absolute private and absolute public," a "liminal space" where social, racial, class and gender boundaries could be broken down and women could be themselves.[16] 'By the 1920s', Thomas Durant Visser outlines, "symbolic connections between the porch and concepts of home and individuality were being recognized" and deemed "liminal places that straddled the realms of privacy and community."[17] While "back porches, with their suggestion of privacy and even secrecy" challenge fictional characters to confront their own ambiguities,[18] the wisteria-covered

---

[15] India Holton, *The Wisteria Society of Lady Scoundrels* (New York: Jove, Penguin Random House, 2021).

[16] Sue Bidwell Beckham, 'The American Front Porch: Women's Liminal Space' (1988) reprinted in Carol Delaney with Deborah Kaspin, *Investigating Culture: An Experiential Introduction to Anthropology* (John Wiley & Sons, Incorporated, 2011), 68-78 (72).

[17] Thomas Durant Visser, *Porches of North America* (Hanover and London: University Press of New England, 2012), 56-7.

[18] Beckham, 'The American Front Porch: Women's Liminal Space', 74.

front house/porch offers female gothic writers with a natural metaphor to suggest the ambiguity that accompanies the concealment of female oppression and domestic abuse. This is most evident in the tales by Gilman and Leahey, where the wisteria adorning the front porch is a conduit for revealing the patriarchal abuse as their female victims adopt the plant's destructive qualities.

Reading Wisteria through an ecoGothic approach

The significance of the wisteria as a gendered metaphor that indicates and reveals domestic abuse is best read through an ecoGothic approach. EcoGothic, according to Andrew Smith and William Hughes, is the exploration of Gothic narratives "through theories of ecocriticism" to "help to critically reinvigorate debate about the class, gender and national identities that inhere within representations of the landscape."[19] Since then, the ecoGothic has become established as the exploration of the interconnectedness of gothic and ecology,[20] and the analysis of the "deep unease, fear, and even contempt" for the natural world even as this is mapped onto "the contours of the body."[21] Using a "distinctive combination of ecocriticism with Gothic and the uncanny, alongside the 'material turn' in cultural theory … [that] encourages a process of critical reinvigoration," Sue Edney's collection of essays develops material ecoGothic methodologies with "an emphasis on the domestic yet liminal space of the garden,"[22] and it is this ecoGothic approach that I use here to illustrate the persistent role of wisteria in women's gothic writing as a metaphor for engaging with the issue of domestic abuse. Blending material ecofeminism with female gothic theories the dichotomy of the wisteria as floral beauty with a penchant for destruction, marks this unusual climbing plant as, what I have called

---

[19] Andrew Smith and William Hughes, 'Introduction: defining the ecoGothic' in *EcoGothic* , edited by Andrew Smith and William Hughes (Manchester: Manchester University Press, 2013), 1-14 (1, 4).

[20] David Del Principe, 'Introduction: The EcoGothic in the Long Nineteenth Century', *Gothic Studies* 16.1 (2014), 1-8.

[21] Dawn Keetley and Matthew Wynn Sivils, 'Introduction: Approaches to the Ecogothic' in *Ecogothic in Nineteenth-Century American Literature*, edited by Dawn Keetley and Matthew Wynn Sivils (New York: Routledge, 2018), 1-20 (4).

[22] Sue Edney, 'Introduction: Phantoms, fantasy and uncanny flowers', in *EcoGothic Gardens in the Long Nineteenth Century*, edited by Sue Edney (Manchester: Manchester University Press, 2020), 1-15 (7).

elsewhere, an eco-*femme fatale*.[23] In dispelling the boundaries of the human and plant through what ecofeminist Stacy Alaimo calls "trans-corporeality," the wisteria itself becomes the "transgressive" female of the phallocentric imagination. Gender and nature become inextricably combined within the wisteria not only as a marker of female oppression and domestic abuse, but in Leahey's tale as a conduit for exacting revenge.

Arguing that the material self is interconnected and inextricable from the wider environment, Stacy Alaimo's trans-corporeality explores various ways in which "the materiality of human bodies and nonhuman natures" is "emerging in many disciplines" such as environmental philosophy, corporeal feminism and transgender theory, to analyse "the entangled territories of material and discursive, natural and cultural, biological and textual."[24] Alaimo focuses on the material transit across human and non-human bodies, charting how the "stuff of matter generates, composes, transforms, and decomposes."[25] "Trans-corporeality," she argues, "not only traces how various substances travel across and within the human body but how they *do* things – often unwelcome or unexpected things" (emphasis in original).[26] Similarly, Nancy Tuana argues that human corporeality and the non-human world are subject to "complex networks of relations" with "permeable and shifting" divisions that reveal "sites of resistance and opposition."[27] Tuana, through her concept of "viscous porosity," asserts that the various social, cultural, political, racial and natural boundaries that establish dualisms, and even skin, flesh or garden fences, are porous membranes through which complex material interactions occur. Both critics explore how nature's material agency affects the human body; how in polluting nature we are polluting ourselves through the material interconnectedness of human and nature. Inverting these concepts within an ecoGothic approach focuses rather on the human material body entering the fictional plant as a (sometimes toxic) body imbuing nature with a gothic supernatural material agency. In both Gilman's and Leahey's tales, the wisteria exemplifies the

---

[23] Teresa Fitzpatrick, 'Green is the new black: Plant monsters as ecoGothic tropes; vampires and *femmes fatales*' in *EcoGothic Gardens in the Long Nineteenth Century*, edited by Sue Edney (Manchester: Manchester University Press, 2020), 130-147.

[24] Alaimo, *Bodily Natures*, 3, 7.

[25] Alaimo, *Bodily Natures*, 143.

[26] Alaimo, *Bodily Natures*, 146.

[27] Nancy Tuana, 'Viscous Porosity: Witnessing Katrina', in *Material Feminisms*, edited by Stacy Alaimo and Susan Hekman (Bloomington: Indiana University Press, 2008), 188-213 (189, 194).

trans-corporeal and the permeable as human and plant matter combine to create an agency of nature that exposes their relevant patriarchal villainy.

Gothic Trans-corporeality in Charlotte Perkins Gilman's 'The Giant Wistaria' (1891)

Charlotte Perkins Gilman was a well-known writer of gothic tales with "feminist themes such as female entrapment and patriarchal control" at the centre of her stories.[28] In this tale, first published in *New England Magazine* in 1891, Gilman draws on gender-nature associations to situate the wisteria as a temporal marker of female repression and domestic abuse. The tale begins in an earlier age of Puritan immigration, opening with a mother's chastisement to her daughter: "Meddle not with my new vine, child! See! Thou hast already broken the tender shoot!" immediately linking the maiden to the delicate young wisteria vine.[29] The reader quickly surmises that Mrs. Dwining's daughter has given birth out of wedlock, resulting in her parents taking the child from her to hide the shame this brings upon the family, and which is the cause of the young woman's restless torture of the young wisteria plant. Indeed, both the young woman's spirit and the wisteria vine shoot are broken in this initial scenario of the New England home. As parental plans to permanently separate the young woman from her child are revealed, the plant mirrors the daughter's anguish at being separated already from her new-born, when the wisteria leaves move "like little stretching fingers" across the oak porch floor as if reaching for the child.[30] The idea is further compounded by the patriarch's association of the wisteria's vigorous growth with the mounting shame his daughter has brought with her to their new community. Of course, such stigma continued into the twentieth century, with specific "sanctuaries" where unwed mothers-to-be were shamefully confined for the duration of their pregnancy and the babies taken for adoption, still operational well into the 1960s.

The narrative quickly switches to the author's present-day as a wealthy couple (George and Jenny) rent the old wisteria-covered house for the summer, along with their respective sisters and brother in-laws. Keen to conjure some ghostly background to their temporary residence that has all

---

[28] Daisy Butcher, in *Evil Roots: Killer Tales of the Botanical Gothic*, edited by Daisy Butcher (London: British Library, 2019), 77.

[29] Charlotte Perkins Gilman, 'The Giant Wistaria' (1891) in *Evil Roots: Killer Tales of the Botanical Gothic*, edited by Daisy Butcher (London: British Library, 2019), 79-88 (79).

[30] Gilman, 'The Giant Wistaria', 79.

but been abandoned by its heirs, the group's attention turns to the massive, twisted wisteria invading the porch. Interest in the supernatural was a popular pastime in the late-nineteenth century, and Jenny's disappointment at the house's lack of haunting or ghost story and all three women's determination that the place is harbouring a spectral presence not only reflects the contemporary moment of whimsy in the face of modernity but reasserts the era's emerging feminism, as the spectral presence often served to highlight repressed wrongs. In turning their attention to the "huge wistaria" covering "the front of the house,"[31] the narrative establishes the proposed repressed haunting as issuing from female / domestic oppression. It is the wistaria that haunts this New England home and exacts the spiritual revenge for the domestic wrongs to its former female inhabitant(s). The now mature plant, that "had once climbed [the porch's] pillars" now "wrenched [the pillars] from their places and [were] held rigid and helpless by the tightly wound and knotted arms,"[32] that suggests a destabilising of patriarchal and domestic structures. The wistaria's floral beauty yet damaging growth of its domestic support structure signifies the duality of domesticity as a safe yet confining female space. Like the young woman within the initial patriarchal household, the domestic structures of the house encourage support and growth, yet although the mature plant and female seek independence from these structures (and strictures), a complete dissolution of these boundaries seems impossible. Moreover, with its "knitted wall of stem and leaf" that "hold[s] up the gutter that had once supported it," and its "drooping, fragrant blossoms made a waving sheet of purple from roof to ground,"[33] the wistaria is at once protective, supportive, and destructive, concealing. Indeed, behind the beautiful floral display lurks a history of female oppression and domestic abuse that the house's new occupants are disposed to discover.

Deciding the damage to the porch by the wisteria is potentially lethal, the tenants organise for the veranda to be repaired – with as little disturbance to the plant as possible. Following up on the spectral imaginings of the night, the "scandal, shame and tragedy" of the Dwining family is revealed when the preserved body of a tiny baby is found in the old well and their workmen find the skeleton of a woman "in the strangling grasp of the roots of the great wistaria."[34] Natania Meeker and Antónia Szabari argue the wisteria's agency in challenging the patriarchal culture that the house and porch represent is a result of the "mother's solicitude for the wisteria" that she is

---

[31] Gilman, 'The Giant Wistaria', 82.
[32] Ibid.
[33] Ibid.
[34] Gilman, 'The Giant Wistaria', 88.

unable to express to her daughter within the confines of the era's patriarchal structures, and which "manifest[s] itself via the plant's arabesque embrace," as "[t]he mother disappears into the plant, and only an affect lingers."[35] While this reading of the plant roots as embracing mother offers a "mode of feminist vegetality,"[36] I argue a trans-corporeal reading offers the wisteria as an ecogothic metaphor that further "imbue[s] the domestic scene with both horror and a destabilizing vitality,"[37] in response to an historic case of domestic violence.

By "[e]mphasizing the material interconnections of human corporeality with the more-than-human world," Alaimo argues, "trans-corporeality also opens up a mobile space that acknowledges the often predictable and unwanted actions of human bodies, nonhuman creatures, ecological systems, chemical agents, and other actors."[38] Gilman's uncanny anthropomorphising of the climber in "The Giant Wistaria" challenges the patriarchal violence towards women that is highlighted through a gothic trans-corporeality. Buried under the liminal space of the porch, whereby the wisteria roots exact a "strangling grasp" of the corpse,[39] reveals, over a century later, the tragic end to the Dwining daughter's transgression and apparent lack of compliance with the patriarchal plan. Applying a trans-corporeal reading to this ecogothic metaphor, the wisteria's absorption of the material body of the daughter provides an uncanny vegetal haunting that sees the wisteria "crawl" up the porch steps "for all the world like a writhing body – cringing - beseeching."[40] Gilman's uncanny descriptions imbue the wisteria with a vegetal agency as it appears to take on the form of the unavenged victim buried within its roots. In a gothic trans-corporeality that sees human and plant merge to enact a bizarre haunting, the wisteria becomes more than a visual symbol of domesticity, or a supernatural tool. Both vegetal and female agency are combined in a clear challenge of patriarchal oppression and domestic violence that serves as a reminder to the contemporary modern characters and readers that despite the social advances of modernity in their privileged circles, female oppression and violence towards women continues to be concealed within the domestic space.

---

[35] Natania Meeker and Antónia Szabari, *Radical Botany: Plants and Speculative Fiction* (New York: Fordham University Press, 2020), 112.
[36] Meeker and Szabari, *Radical Botany*, 113.
[37] Meeker and Szabari, *Radical Botany*, 113.
[38] Alaimo, *Bodily Natures*, 2.
[39] Gilman, 'The Giant Wistaria', 88.
[40] Gilman, 'The Giant Wistaria', 83.

Trans-corporeal body horror in Donna A. Leahey's 'The Wisteria' (2014)

In a twenty-first century re-working of Gilman's tale, Donna A. Leahey upgrades the wisteria as a gendered Gothic metaphor for domestic abuse through an uncanny body horror that discards the human-nature divide. In "The Wisteria" (2014),[41] a tale with a distinct feminist vibe, the monstrous merging of human and vegetal re-visits and re-conceptualises gendered nature through a trans-corporeal mutation that demonstrates a "becoming-plant" that Karen Houle suggests involves more than a shared experience, but rather is a "heterogenous alliance" with the vegetal.[42] Leahey's vengeful wisteria exhibits a trans-corporeal alliance that creates a monstrous plant-human hybrid through ecoGothic body horror. Body horror of the post-millennium focuses on "anxieties surrounding transformation, mutation and contagion" of the body,[43] that a gothic trans-corporeal commingling of human and plant illustrate in a physical form. Such monsters, according to Jeffrey Jerome Cohen, depict "those who overstep the boundaries of their gender roles or assigned sexual identity."[44] The material and visceral trans-corporeal human-plant transformation in Leahey's tale uses the wisteria as a physical manifestation of ecoGothic body horror to underline the contemporary issues of domestic abuse and violence against women. As Gina Wisker asserts, "Postfeminist Gothic ... revitalises feminism's broader issues, including gender equality, inclusivity and diversity' through 'reimagine[d] familiar Gothic figures," inevitably encompassing contemporary "[v]iolence and oppression."[45] By including the plant as a gendered protagonist, Leahey re-works the wisteria as a trans-corporeal ecoGothic metaphor for the twenty-first century.

---

[41] Donna A. Leahey, 'The Wisteria', in *Growing Concerns*, edited by Alex Hurst (Fort Smith, AR: Chupa Cabra House, 2014), 9-20.

[42] Karen F. Houle, 'Animal, Vegetable, Mineral: Ethics as Extension or Becoming? The Case of Becoming- Plant', *Journal for Critical Animal Studies*, IX.1/2 (2011), 89-116 (97). [last accessed: 21/08/2018].

[43] Xavier Aldana Reyes, *Body Gothic: Corporeal Transgression in Contemporary Literature and Horror Film* (Cardiff: University of Wales Press, 2014), 54.

[44] Jeffrey Jerome Cohen, 'Monster Culture (Seven Theses)', in *The Monster Theory Reader*, edited by Jeffrey Andrew Weinstock (Minneapolis: University of Minnesota Press, 2020), 37-57 (42).

[45] Gina Wisker, 'Postfeminist Gothic', in *Twenty-First-Century Gothic: An Edinburgh Companion*, edited by Maisha Wester and Xavier Aldana Reyes (Edinburgh: Edinburgh University Press, 2019), 47-59 (51-2).

The tale begins with a domestic argument about the potential damage the 5-year-old wisteria is doing to the siding and deck of the couple's house as the tendrils are "stretching towards the roof ... as if the plant were trying to get into the house."[46] Like Gilman, Leahey imbues the wisteria with vegetal agency through anthropomorphic description that suggests intent. She observes with growing unease how the wisteria vines were "reaching and exploring ... as if the plant were attacking the house."[47] The female narrator (Gia) reveals that for her, the wisteria "had seemed symbolic of [her] resurrected marriage" after her college professor husband's numerous affairs with his graduate assistants appears to end when his most overt tryst with Melissa results in her leaving abruptly.[48] However, while the wisteria grows as if it has "found a bag of Miracle-Gro," Gia's marriage continues to disintegrate.[49] The violent undercurrent of their verbal exchanges suggest a level of verbal and emotional domestic abuse from husband Charles, as he threatens to kill the wisteria and her pet dog. The domestic violence plays out through the husband's missing cat, found under the deck, entangled in the mass of wisteria vines and covered in blood. In this tale of terror Leahey emphasises the material interconnectedness of trans-corporeality and the wisteria's vegetal agency when Gia struggles to free the cat. Armed with garden shears, Gia notes that as soon as she "cut the first vine, Snowbelle [the cat] shrieked to life" as if Gia had "cut her and not an inanimate plant."[50] Of course, plants are far from inanimate, but in exaggerating a vegetal vitality when Gia attempts to pull the cat free and "the resistance was strong enough that it feels as if the vines were pulling back,"[51] Leahey develops the wisteria beyond a mere symbol for domesticity towards acknowledging a vegetal agency that draws on a female monstrous Other – "a menacing alterity of the natural environment" at the heart of ecophobia.[52] For Simon C. Estok, ecophobia is the perceived threat of the nonhuman world that holds "imagined challenges to our existence," evoking fears "about the transience of our corporeal materiality," revealed in the "contempt and fear we feel for the agency of the natural environment."[53] When Gia ecophobically

---

[46] Leahey, 'The Wisteria', 10.
[47] Leahey, 'The Wisteria', 13.
[48] Leahey, 'The Wisteria', 12.
[49] Leahey, 'The Wisteria', 10.
[50] Leahey, 'The Wisteria', 14.
[51] Leahey, 'The Wisteria', 14.
[52] Simon C. Estok, 'Painful Material Realities, Tragedy, Ecophobia', in *Material ecocriticism*, edited by Serenella Iovino and Serpil Oppermann (Bloomington: Indiana University Press, 2014), 130-140 (130).
[53] Estok, 'Painful Material Realities, Tragedy, Ecophobia', 131.

prunes the vine to access its roots, the wisteria's trans-corporeal monstrosity is demonstrated when a "thick red liquid dripped down" around the narrator "as warm as blood" until the deck resembles "a murder scene," which it indeed turns out to be.[54]

While Gilman's characters experience ghostly imaginings that result in the discovery of a skeleton, Leahey's tale recognises vegetal agency and trans-corporeal horror in Gia's exposure of Melissa's human skeleton buried under the deck, stripped of its material flesh and blood by the vine. Wisteria and corpse actively merge as "a skeletal hand pushed out of the earth … At the same time, vines and leaves wrapped themselves around the bones, weaving themselves about, forming the shape of a human arm" eventually becoming a recognisable effigy of Charles' former mistress.[55] As "[i]nch by inch the skeleton dragged itself out of the dirt like a flower blooming in the sun," the wisteria vines "swirled around the skeleton filling out a woman's shape, covering her skull to give her a face with a skin of smooth leaves and eyes of purple flowers."[56] The ecoGothic body horror of Leahey's contemporary version of the wisteria emphasises a material commingling of plant-human as the vine, having trans-corporcally absorbed the body's flesh, creates a liminal yet physical revenant through the living plant re-forming around the skeletal structure. The vine actively keeps the figure of Melissa together, even when Gia's dog runs off with a leg bone during the vegetal form's attack on his owner as the vegetal revenant seeks Charles. A trans-corporeal monster, the Melissa-wisteria demonstrates both vegetal and female agency as it takes revenge for the woman's brutal murder and ultimately freeing Gia from her destructive marriage.

When Charles traps Gia against the wall threateningly on her discovery of his murder of Melissa, who became inconvenient to him when she became pregnant, the transformed plant-human monster enacts reprisal for the physical abuse suffered in human form. Wrapping itself around Charles, "her skeletal mouth and vine lips closed onto his," as the wisteria-woman begins to drag him towards her grave "as vines erupted out of his body."[57] The horror stems, not only in the unsettling trans-corporeality of the female gendered vine, but in a "becoming-plant" that serves to remind us of the power of nature over man. Although Jack Halberstam argues that monsters

---

[54] Leahey, 'The Wisteria', 16.
[55] Ibid.
[56] Leahey, 'The Wisteria', 17.
[57] Leahey, 'The Wisteria', 19.

"can represent gender, race, nationality, class and sexuality in one body,"[58] Leahey's tale offers the wisteria as an ecoGothic metaphor for a contemporary feminist dialogue of domestic abuse and oppression. The ultimate combining of vengeful woman with the female-associated plant brings this wisteria as eco-*femme fatale* into the twenty-first century.

Bibliography

Alaimo, Stacy. 2010. *Bodily Natures: Science, Environment and the Material Self*, Bloomington and Indianapolis: Indiana University Press.

Aldana Reyes, Xavier. 2014. *Body Gothic: Corporeal Transgression in Contemporary Literature and Horror Film*, Cardiff: University of Wales Press.

Bidwell Beckham, Sue. 1988. 'The American Front Porch: Women's Liminal Space' reprinted in Delaney Carol with Kaspin, Deborah. 2011. *Investigating Culture: An Experiential Introduction to Anthropology*, John Wiley & Sons, Incorporated: 68-78.

Butcher, Daisy. ed. 2019. *Evil Roots: Killer Tales of the Botanical Gothic*, London: British Library.

Cohen, Jeffrey Jerome. 2020. 'Monster Culture (Seven Theses)', in *The Monster Theory Reader*, edited by Jeffrey Andrew Weinstock. Minneapolis: University of Minnesota Press: 37-57.

Craciun, Adriana. 2009. *Fatal Women of Romanticism,* Cambridge: Cambridge University Press

Del Principe, David. 'Introduction: The EcoGothic in the Long Nineteenth Century', *Gothic Studies* 16.1 (2014), 1-8.

Durant Visser, Thomas. 2012. *Porches of North America*, Hanover and London: University Press of New England.

Edney, Sue. 2020. 'Introduction: Phantoms, fantasy and uncanny flowers', in *EcoGothic Gardens in the Long Nineteenth Century*, edited by Sue Edney. Manchester: Manchester University Press: 1-15.

Estok, Simon C. 2014. 'Painful Material Realities, Tragedy, Ecophobia', in *Material ecocriticism*, edited by Serenella Iovino and Serpil Oppermann. Bloomington: Indiana University Press: 130-140.

Fitzpatrick, Teresa. 2020. 'Green is the new black: Plant monsters as ecoGothic tropes; vampires and *femmes fatales*' in *EcoGothic Gardens*

---

[58] Jack Halberstam, 'Parasites and Perverts: An Introduction to Gothic Monstrosity', in *The Monster Theory Reader*, edited by Jeffrey Andrew Weinstock (Minneapolis: University of Minnesota Press, 2020), 148-173 (165).

in the Long Nineteenth Century, edited by Sue Edney. Manchester: Manchester University Press: 130-147.

Garrard, Greg. 2004. *Ecocriticism,* Oxon: Routledge.

Gilman, Charlotte Perkins. 1891. 'The Giant Wistaria' in *Evil Roots: Killer Tales of the Botanical Gothic*, edited by Daisy Butcher. London: British Library: 79-88.

Grasser, Celine. 2005. "Good Girls versus Blooming Maidens: The Building of Female Middle- and Upper-Class Identities in the Garden, England and France, 1820-1870", in *Secret Gardens, Satanic Mills: Placing Girls in European History, 1750-1960*, ed. by Mary Jo Maynes, Birgitte Soland & Christina Benninghaus. Bloomington: Indiana University Press: 131-146.

Halberstam, Jack. 2020. 'Parasites and Perverts: An Introduction to Gothic Monstrosity', in *The Monster Theory Reader*, edited by Jeffrey Andrew Weinstock. Minneapolis: University of Minnesota Press: 148-173.

Holton, India. 2021. *The Wisteria Society of Lady Scoundrels*, New York: Jove, Penguin Random House.

Houle, Karen F. 'Animal, Vegetable, Mineral: Ethics as Extension or Becoming? The Case of Becoming- Plant', *Journal for Critical Animal Studies*, IX.1/2 (2011), 89-116.

Hughes, William. 2020. 'Foreword: On the Gothic nature of gardens', in *EcoGothic Gardens in the Long Nineteenth Century: Phantoms, Fantasy and Uncanny Flowers*, ed. by Sue Edney, Manchester: Manchester University Press: pp.xiv-xvii.

Hurley, Kelly. 1996. *The Gothic Body,* Cambridge: Cambridge University Press.

Johnston, Elizabeth. 'The Original 'Nasty Woman'', *The Atlantic*, 6 November 2016

Keetley, Dawn and Wynn Sivils, Matthew. 2018. 'Introduction: Approaches to the Ecogothic' in *Ecogothic in Nineteenth-Century American Literature*, edited by Dawn Keetley and Matthew Wynn Sivils. New York: Routledge: 1-20.

Leahey, Donna A. 2014. 'The Wisteria', in *Growing Concerns*, edited by Alex Hurst. Fort Smith, AR: Chupa Cabra House: 9-20.

Meeker Natania and Szabari, Antónia. 2020. *Radical Botany: Plants and Speculative Fiction,* New York: Fordham University Press.

Murphy, Bernice M. 2009. *The Suburban Gothic in American Popular Culture*, Basingstoke: Palgrave Macmillan.

Royal Horticultural Society website:
https://www.rhs.org.uk/search?query=wisteria

Smith, Andrew and Hughes, William. 2013. 'Introduction: defining the ecoGothic' in *EcoGothic* edited by Andrew Smith and William Hughes. Manchester: Manchester University Press: 1-14.

Stott, Rebecca. 1992. *The Fabrication of the Late-Victorian Femme Fatale: The Kiss of Death,* Basingstoke and London: MacMillan Press Ltd.

Tuana, Nancy. 2008. 'Viscous Porosity: Witnessing Katrina', in *Material Feminisms*, edited by Stacy Alaimo and Susan Hekman. Bloomington: Indiana University Press: 188-213.

Waters, Michael. 1988. *The Garden in Victorian Literature*, Aldershot: Scholar Press.

Wisker, Gina. 2019. 'Postfeminist Gothic', in *Twenty-First-Century Gothic: An Edinburgh Companion*, edited by Maisha Wester and Xavier Aldana Reyes. Edinburgh: Edinburgh University Press: 47-59.

CHAPTER THREE

TRANSCENDING THE URBAN:
THE QUEEN OF SHEBA[1]

AMANDA BELL

Speaking in Enniskillen, Northern Ireland in August 2013, Kathleen Jamie remarked that her interest in writing about the natural world began a decade ago, a reference to the 2004 publication of *The Tree House*, her first overtly ecopoetic collection, and her turn towards what has come to be called "the new nature writing": her award-winning collections *Findings* (2005) and *Sightlines* (2012).[2] However, the seeds of her ecological sensibility are evident in the 1994 collection *The Queen of Sheba*, which can be seen as the beginning of her mature work. Interviewed by Belinda McKeon for *The Irish Times* in 2005, Jamie expressed some regret at having her juvenilia in the public domain, wishing that instead of starting her publishing career so early she had "arrive[d] on the scene at thirty-three." Written at this juncture, *The Queen of Sheba*, noted for its "various forensic critiques of modern Scotland,"[3] also marks the first stages of Jamie's interrogation of the place of the human in the world. How this develops in the course of the collection can be seen as a paradigm for the development of an ecopoetics.

The Queen of Sheba appeared at an important moment in the raising of environmental awareness in Scotland. In 1990, the Scottish Green Party had separated from the UK Greens, and saw its membership surge from under 100 members to 1250.[4] In 1995, The Environment Act (UK) made provision for the establishment of the Scottish Environment Protection Agency the following year. Perhaps most significantly in terms of impact on the public

---

[1] Republished with permission from Edinburgh University Press volume, *Kathleen Jamie: Essays and Poems on Her Work.*
[2] Kathleen Jamie in conversation with Tim Dee, 'Alone with Nature', *Happy Days Enniskillen International Beckett Festival,* 22-26 August 2013.
[3] Neil, 'History in a new scheme', 2000.
[4] Kuin, p. 138.

imagination, early in January 1993 the Liberian-registered oil tanker *MV Braer* ran aground off the Shetland Islands, spilling almost all of her cargo of 84,000 tonnes of light crude oil into the sea, with catastrophic implications for both wildlife and the fishing and tourism industries.[5] The spill was twice the volume of that lost from the Exxon Valdez in 1989. There was a strong volunteer response to the disaster, as local people braved the adverse weather conditions to rescue dead and dying seabirds and animals. Jamie's devastation at the event is recorded in her notebook from that year: "Wreck of the Braer at Shetland / wretched, despair. / 'Only when we have been truly heartbroken can we be whole' [...] After pain comes a security / wish for a new / seawashed / spirituality."[6] Against this backdrop, *The Queen of Sheba*, in its struggle to determine what an ecological worldview might entail, captures both a personal turning point, and the zeitgeist.

The collection is characterized by juxtapositions, which operate as heuristic devices in working towards an understanding of the gnarly relationship of the human to the nonhuman world, and of the role of the poet in portraying this dynamic. The struggle played out in these poems operates as what Josephine Donovan, in a collection of ecofeminist essays published in the same year, calls "a vehicle for the revelation of being, rather than a mechanism for its domination."[7] The concept that, by revealing being, literature can reawaken awareness about the relationship of the human to the nonhuman is familiar from the work of ecocritic Jonathan Bate, who describes the role of *ecopoesis* as being to "engage *imaginatively* with the non-human." [8]

The Queen of Sheba implicitly problematizes the idea of "nature poetry" or "ecopoetry" by questioning the concepts of nature and ecology, much as ecocriticism itself has done. As the collection progresses, Jamie sets up a series of dualisms: between east and west, exotic Arabia and astringent Presbyterianism in the title poem, the old and the new, age and youth in "Mr and Mrs Scotland are Dead"; travel and return in "Coupie" and "Rooms"; freedom and domesticity in "Wee Baby" and "Wee Wifey"; modernity and prehistory in "One of Us." The overarching dualism in the collection is that of urban and rural, which she uses to represent different aspects of the constraints facing a young woman wrestling with the idea of how to be in the world.

---

[5] Marine Accident Investigation Branch Report. Ironically, the wreck of the *MV Braer* is now itself marketed as a tourist attraction for scuba divers, promoted on the official site for Shetland tourism.

[6] Jamie, 'Literary Papers', Accession 11599/8, pp. 41-42.

[7] Donovan, 'Ecofeminist Literary Criticism', p. 88.

[8] Bate, *Song of the Earth,* p. 199.

Threaded through the collection are poems which chart the growth of a female sensibility, sometimes in the first person, sometimes in the second, from childhood through early parenthood and into independent self-awareness. The attainment of self-awareness coincides with an enriched understanding of the human relationship to the environment. In this paradigm, the urban is represented by the constructed human environment and the rules for normative behaviour; the rural by the natural, nonhuman, world outside. Jamie's idea of "rural" does not conform to the essentialist Romantic concept of unpopulated space, but rather represents a sought-after alternative to the reality of lived urban experience, an exploration of the trope, common in popular culture, that "there must be more to life than this." The rural mutates according to circumstance, but always comes with the alluring idea that there must be something better, something beyond the judgemental, impoverishing restrictions of sexism, constructed environments, social constraints, and the language which articulates them. The desire for the rural, or wilderness, is an appeal to the authority of nature, a search for the ecosublime, and the concomitant search for an originary language represents a desire to transcend political affiliation, to be identified on one's own terms.[9] Questioned throughout her career about the influence of gender and nationality on her work, Jamie has described herself as being a poet not *because* she is Scottish and a woman, but affected by the fact that she is. The struggle towards poetic voice incorporates an examination of whether language and landscape can be without political connotation: the mutating concepts of urban and rural become tools employed in this search.

The constantly shifting aspect of the urban-rural dualism is central to *The Queen of Sheba*.[10] Juxtapositions of these in the Scottish context could be seen to represent the landed wealthy and the impoverished crofters or migrants of the industrial revolution. The urban could be seen as a dystopian condition, in contrast to the idyll of rural living, though in contemporary societies, albeit more in the USA than Britain and Ireland, cities are frequently seen as a civilizing counterpart to degraded rustic life.[11] In *The Queen of Sheba*, rural is neither a traditional agrarian way of life, nor the wilderness conceived of by American transcendentalism, and certainly not

---

[9] Rozelle defines the 'ecosublime' as 'the awe and terror that occurs when literary figures experience the infinite complexity and contingency of place', *Ecosublime,* p. 1.

[10] On the complex interrelationship between the concepts 'urban' and 'rural' in Scotland today see Scott et al., 'The Urban Rural Divide'.

[11] Ross, 'The Social Claim on Urban Ecology', p. 24.

the politically fraught spaces of land-cleared estates, but a prismatic concept best thought of as the "anti-urban."[12]

The impulse behind constructing these dichotomies demonstrates the poet's accelerating struggle to transcend inherited constraints and charts the ever-strengthening lure of the non-human world as part of a maturation process. Looking at this process as it unfolds in the course of the collection, focusing on "Mother-May-I", "A Shoe", "Child with pillar box and bin bags", "Fountain", "All washed up", "Flashing green man", "At Point of Ness" and "Skeins o Geese", it is evident that the mutating urban-rural dualism is used in each one to represent different aspects of the struggle for voice and identity. These poems dealing with central aspects of female experience constitute a core coming-of-age narrative of environmental encounter.

"Mother-May-I" is exemplary in its establishment of multiple dualisms. Written in the voice of an urban child living near the edge of a housing scheme, and longing to escape it and flee to the woods and the wild, the poem proceeds like an inventory of obstacles to achieving this: the urban is used here to represent constraints of age, gender and normative behaviour. Mother-May-I is a children's game where the players are entirely in the power of the 'mother' figure, sometimes also called "Captain" or "Mr Wolf", and have to ask permission for anything they want to do. It is in the power of the "mother" to grant or deny the request, to specify how it should be done, or to impose an entirely different task on the asker. The convention of the game introduces the idea of disempowerment, a disempowerment in conflict with the huge ambition of the child. The child's requests in the poem start as small and reasonable, with a wish to go as far as the end of the lane, but rapidly become more daring and dangerous. The next request is to "leave these lasses games/ and play at Man-hunt" (*QS* 12). Man-hunt is a children's game of tag, but the capitalization and hyphenation of the word, and the fact that this request comes straight after the description of the woods as a site of criminality and perversion, populated by anonymous child molesters, gives a sinister overtone to the game, evocative of the chase in William Golding's *Lord of the Flies*, and confirming that children's games function as an analogue for adult behaviour. The next question, seeking permission to 'tell small lies', proceeds along the continuum towards adulthood. The final request, "Mother may we/ pull our soft backsides/ through the jagged may's/ white blossom" suggests a rite – literally of passage – which could represent either a social initiation, such as

---

[12] Gairn's discussion of 'Scottish literary technophobia' is illuminating on the division between the portrayal of the urban and the rural in post-WWII Scotland. See Gairn, *Ecology and Modern Scottish Literature*, pp. 110-55.

communion, confirmation, or marriage; or an experiential initiation, such as puberty, loss of virginity, or childbirth (*QS* 12). The narrator is hungry to experience the outside world, not the enclosed teenage world of discos and cinemas, but the wilderness of the burn and the woods, which she associates with freedom.

What is constraining the child from exploring the woods? First, the rules of the game – the need to request and be granted permission; second, the urban legends, rumours of paedophiles and perverts which have just enough grounding in reality to be plausible – discarded pornography leading on to rumours of mouldering corpses and missing hitch-hikers. The use of myth to warn children, and particularly female children, away from exploration and possible transgression has its origins in medieval folk tales, but Jamie subverts the trope of the conventional antithesis between the safe town or village and the dangerous woods by ending the poem with the child's glee at attaining the superficially simple yet metaphorically significant pleasure of seeing the white dye from her gym shoes dissolve and run downstream.[13] By confronting the myths propagated about the world beyond the suburb, the child has attained a primal pleasure.

A third constraint on the child's explorations is that of clothing – the impractical skirts and dresses which hamper the activity of little girls by fanning out in the dirt, the white gym-shoes which need to be kept clean. Fourth, the physical obstacle of the dump – the detritus of the city that forms a barrier between the built environment and what lies outside it. This could be the same "civic amenity landfill site" which provides the setting for "Mr and Mrs Scotland are dead": a liminal space composed of the city's waste but overlaid with reminders of another way of being, as Mr Scotland's puncture repair kit, abandoned among the detritus, evokes memories of "hedgerows/ hanged with small black brambles' hearts" (*QS* 37). The choice of the dump as a defining liminal space between urban and rural in "Mother-May-I" has resonances in the objects out of place that feature throughout the collection: the platform on the beach in "A Shoe" (*QS* 13), the washed-up form in "Another day in paradise" (*QS* 56): pieces of flotsam which spark a meditation on the impact of the human in the wider world.

---

[13] The use of the cautionary tale was formalized in seventeenth century France by Charles Perrault's fairy tales, notably *Le Petit Chaperon Rouge,* and recurs throughout European fairy tales from the Grimm Brothers' German tales to those documented by Italo Calvino in 20th century Italy. Pullman points out how such tales are resuscitated during periods of heightened anxiety about paedophilia and 'stranger danger' (p. 142), now ubiquitous thanks to prurient media outlets. Kossick has noted Jamie's 'indebtedness to the baroque textual strategies of Angela Carter' in this poem, in 'Roaring Girls, Bogie Wives', p. 201.

Dumps in *The Queen of Sheba* are morally neutral environments, holding areas where objects await triage, dispensed with not for intrinsic uselessness, but for having outlived their usefulness.[14] In "Findings", Jamie notes that on the Monach islands, "a 21st century midden of aerosols and plastic bottles," what the beachcombers chose to keep was "not the things that endured, but those that were transformed by death or weather." (*F* 66) In the era of plastic, durability has ceased to be positive attribute, and the concept of disposability provides a strong starting point for a meditation on the human relationship to the environment.

So, on the one side are rules, myths, conventions, barriers; on the other a powerful desire for escape and experience, both geographical and maturational. The transcendence of four types of urban constraint, conceived of in this poem as a loss of innocence – is a source of huge delight, and the double meaning of the last word in the phrase 'muck about at the woods and burn' lends a sacramental aspect to the child's achievement: the transcendence is itself a rite, a trial by fire.

The possibilities of escape to the anti-urban are fewer in "Child with pillar box and bin bags." The focus in this poem is on a young mother, and the paraphernalia of parenthood, both physical and emotional, proves a more powerful deterrent to connecting with the nonhuman world than the obstacles facing the small girl in the earlier poem. Lacking the egocentric ferocity of childhood, the young woman has more fear, and therefore less perceived choice. To photograph her baby, she chooses the side of the street "dark in the shade of the tenements" (*QS* 15). The tenements, the buildings, the bookies, though indicative of the crowded life of an urban proletariat, are not in themselves intimidating, they are neutral, "friendly buildings", and the implication is that they too have a type of life – "the traffic ground, the buildings shook, the baby breathed": this is not a simplistic juxtaposition of the sun as a representation of nature and all things good versus buildings representing the urban and all things bad, but rather an awareness of choice – it is possible to choose the sun and its fascinating shadows. Fear for the baby's safety, "fearful as Niagara", seems to eliminate the possibility of recognizing that choice exists – "if she'd chosen or thought it possible to choose." The use of "Niagara" as a simile for the kerb indicates a terror of

---

[14] Bardini defines junk as something which 'used to be useful, to serve a purpose, or … was meant to eventually serve a purpose. Its time is always in between, a bubble in the efficient, productive time we unfortunately enough got hooked on in the so-called developed world. Junk lives in a time stasis. Junk is a luxury for the well fed; it incarnates the sentimental scrap we choose to love tenderly in these parts of the world. It materializes the memories of consumption that we grew up idolizing.' *Junkware*, p. 9.

natural phenomena – surely if a child's buggy is rolling off a kerb fear should be of traffic, the kerb itself, the hard road, but all of the terrors for the child are embodied in the image of a world-renowned geological feature. The most potent obstacle to the young woman who is the subject of this poem is fear – a societally engendered fear of the world outside of the constructed environment.

This sense of powerlessness to recognise choice, particularly once the subject is constrained by the demands of parenthood, is further developed in "Fountain." Young parents, and from the line "who these days can thrust her wrists / into a giggling hillside spring" we can infer that these young parents are overwhelmingly female, are caught in a manmade theme-park, a shopping mall full of escalators and hard surfaces, where everything is artificial: plastic bags, polystyrene cups, perspex foliage, neon signs (*QS* 17). There is, nevertheless, something else, should people choose to see or feel it. The question "who these days can thrust her wrists into a giggling hillside spring above some ancient city" seems rhetorical, raising once more the question of choice. The next question, "who says we can't respond...", implies that the spring, as symbol of the natural world beyond the machine, is accessible to all, whether they know it or not. The reference to Virgil's *Eclogues* is a reminder of the enduring draw of the anti-urban for humankind, but in this poem the anti-urban is simmering below concrete surfaces, ready to erupt. The incongruity of the Arcadian well in the shopping centre relates back to "A Shoe," which takes elements from both the manufactured realm and the natural world, and places them in the opposing environment: thus, we find the thick sole of a platform shoe among pebbles on the beach, and on the bathroom shelf a collection of "pretty/ Queeny shells" (*QS* 13). This superficially humorous mixing of register and context gives way to a sobering contemplation: how did the wearer of the shoe feel? Did she jump off the bridge, or rather choose to walk into the sea? The penultimate stanza poses a profound question, "did she walk in, saying yes/ I recognise this/ as the water yanked heavy/ on thighs belly breasts?" This sense, or act, of recognition is pivotal to the collection – a connection to a point of origin, a return to the primordial. An unnerving blend of humour and gravitas, "A Shoe" is a rallying call to engage on a deeper level with existence, with the reassurance that "it's all right/ once you're out the other side."

There is a dual aspect to the urban-rural dynamic in the collection. Those within the city feel, with mounting intensity, the draw of the anti-urban, whereas those portrayed as external to the constructed environment feel it as a threat, a symbol of destruction. In 'All Washed Up' the city is a metaphor for ruin and dereliction – emotional as much as physical. The foundering relationship, described in terms of shipwreck, is pronounced dead by invocation of the city. Clearly the city here is an emotional and imaginative space rather than a physical location: it is "far from any shore," simultaneously land-locked and cast adrift (*QS* 35). Increasingly as the collection progresses, there is an intimation of life just within reach of the constructed environment, be it underground or overhead. In "Fountain" it is intuited by the twitch of the dowser's rod in the baby's buggy; in 'Flashing green man' it is signaled by the geese flying overhead. The voice in "Flashing green man" is that of an urbanite, "one of the city" (*QS* 38). The flashing green man, "he too refuged in cities", is a constant reminder of what lies beyond, an avatar of the geese themselves. The image first conjured by the calling geese is that of "ancient contraptions / abandoned on farms", a salute to rural depopulation and nineteenth- and twentieth-century migration to industrial centres. But the geese are also a reminder of how close the countryside is in the present moment, as they "pull themselves North to the Sidlaws": this is not a huge sprawling metropolis, but a small city near to the mountains. There is a sense here, just over halfway through the collection, of breakthrough: the geese are a "true sign", their wings "more precious than angels." Although the portents of the nonhuman world are stronger in this poem, they need to be – the cumulative effect of adulthood and city-living have deadened the senses: this state of adulthood, being "one of the city," involves taking "little time to consider," an emotional and sensory numbness. In contrast to this unreflective life, the moment of noticing the geese, gilded with sunlight reflected against windows, is characterized by stillness: the poet stands transfixed while people and traffic stream around her, everything else is movement: "and people flowed around me / intent on home; from the roundabout's hub / traffic wheeled off to the suburbs." The trope of mindfulness, of taking time to consider, spools through the collection, from the sense of recognition in "A Shoe" to the absence of time to consider in "Flashing green man," to a moment of epiphany in "At Point of Ness", which is discussed below.

From the restless child of "Mother-May-I" through the young women in "Child with pillar box and bin bags" and "Fountain", the urban-rural relationship has become less dichotomous, the two facets of being are beginning to overlap: by "Flashing green man" the voices of the geese bring the rural – past and present – into the city, anticipated by their avatar the flashing green man: they are accessible harbingers of an alternative way of being.[15] It is a paradigm for the increasing acceptance of the interconnection

---

[15] In 'Flashing Green Man' the geese encapsulate nostalgia for the past, the sense of being in the moment, and a harbinger of a utopian future, thereby fulfilling the three orientations of pastoral – elegy, idyll and utopia – discussed by Garrard, pp. 37-38.

of all aspects of existence central to an ecopoetic worldview. It can be argued that the shift in focus to a true ecopoetic impulse occurs at the end of the collection, between "At Point of Ness" and "Skeins o geese." The former, in its epiphanic assertion that "heart-scared, I have it/ understood:/ *never ever/ harm — this, / you never could*," uses a didactic form of statement of intent (*QS* 62). By the final poem, this conviction has been transformed into an attempt to make language itself, rather than words, articulate how it is to dwell in the world, mindful of the inherent contradictions of such an approach.

"Skeins o geese" picks up directly on the theme of "Flashing green man." The image of a stationary figure at the centre of milling activity in "Flashing green man" is evocative of the time-lapse sequences in Godfrey Reggio's *Koyaanisqatski*, the cult film described as a visual tone poem, which depicts multiplicitous interactions between humans, nature and technology. The analogy between 'Flashing green man' and *Koyaanisqatski* is illuminating in terms of Jamie's representation of the geese in 'Skeins o geese'. Godfrey Reggio explained his decision not to have dialogue in the trilogy of films beginning with *Koyaanisqatski* by stating that "it's not for lack of love of language, but because I feel our language is in a state of vast humiliation, I decided to make films without words." [16] The same sense of the inadequacy of language to express the natural world is doubly indicated in 'Skeins o geese'. The word written by the geese is both everlasting and unattainable: "Skeins o geese write a word/ across the sky. A word/ struck lik a gong/ afore I wis born." (*QS* 64) The gong, Tibetan singing bowl or *rin gong*, continues at too high a frequency to be audible. Like the word, it "whustles/ ower high for ma senses." The meaning is there, but how can it be accessed? In describing both the inaccessibility of the geese's communication, and the straining towards the nonhuman involved in trying to comprehend it, the poem enacts *ecopoesis* by imaginative engagement with the non-human, evoking George Mackay Brown's edict for poets to "carve the runes / then be content with silence." [17] The conundrum is partly answered by the shift into blended Scots. J. Derrick McClure, in *Why Scots Matters*, notes that:

> in the principal English-speaking countries, the language, in its spoken and written forms, is increasingly limited to its simplest, least imaginative and least challenging registers. Its utilitarian use as a language of technology, commerce, tourism and mass entertainment has undermined its status as a vehicle for work of literary and intellectual distinction; and the sheer

---

[16] In *Essence of Life*, directed by Greg Carson, 2002.
[17] George Mackay Brown, 'A Work for Poets'.

quantity of dross produced in the language makes it progressively more difficult for work of merit to receive widespread attention.[18]

It is particularly noteworthy then that Jamie shifts into Scots to articulate this straining towards connection with the nonhuman world: to truly transcend the constraints hitherto represented by the urban-rural dichotomy, it may also be necessary to transcend the official language. This appropriation of language reflects the work pattern of Hugh MacDiarmid, who, as Louisa Gairn notes, felt that "synthetic Scots was the only idiom [...] capable of representing the complex entanglements of man and environment in the modern world."[19]

In the course of *The Queen of Sheba* Jamie has interrogated the possibilities of language, from the biblical to the inarticulable. The difficulty of finding a language reflects the difficulty of transcending the urban. Jamie has grappled with the idea of not using language at all, before concluding that language is what, as humans, we do best. By moving away from English, she is taking a step towards freeing herself from the constraints heretofore represented by constructed environments. Her switch into Scots as a literary language represents a reclaiming of linguistic biodiversity, a cogent demonstration of the power of literature to take tangible action in defense of a biosphere increasingly under threat.

Bibliography

Bardini, Thierry. 2011. *Junkware* (Minneapolis: University of Minnesota Press.

Bate, Jonathan. 2000. *The Song of the Earth.* London: Picador.

Brown, George Mackay. 1996. 'A Work for Poets', *Following a Lark.* London: John Murray Ltd. http://www.georgemackaybrown.co.uk/extracts%20from/WorkforPoets.htm [accessed 27 Jan 2014].

Donovan, Josephine. 1994. 'Ecofeminist Literary Criticism: Reading the Orange', in Gaard and Murphy (eds.), *Ecofeminist Literary Criticism.* Urbana and Chicago: University of Illinois Press.

Essence of Life, The, film. 2002. Directed by Greg Carson. USA: MGM Home Entertainment.

Gairn, Louisa. 2008. *Ecology and Modern Scottish Literature.* Edinburgh: Edinburgh University Press.

---

[18] McClure, *Why Scots Matters*, p. 66-67.
[19] Gairn, *Ecology*, p. 82.

Garrard, Greg. 2004. *Ecocriticism.* London: Routledge.
Golding, William. 1954. *Lord of the Flies.* London: Faber and Faber.
Jamie, Kathleen. 2005. *Findings.* London: Sort of Books.
—. 'Literary Papers 1980-97. Accession 11599.' National Library of Scotland.
—. *Sightlines.* 2012. London: Sort of Books.
—. *The Queen of Sheba.* 1994. Newcastle upon Tyne: Bloodaxe Books.
—. *The Tree House.* 2004. London: Picador, 2004.
Kossick, Kay. 2001. 'Roaring Girls, Bogie Wives, and the Queen of Sheba: Dissidence, Desire and Dreamwork in the Poetry of Kathleen Jamie.' In *Studies in Scottish Literature* 32, 1 (2001), 195-212.
Koyaanisqatski, film 1983. Directed by Godfrey Reggio. USA: Island Alive /New Cinema.
Kuin, Inger. 2006. 'Review: Green Party Membership.' In *Scottish Affairs* 55, 138-41 www.scottishaffairs.org/backiss/pdfs/sa55/Sa55_Kuin.pdf [accessed 3 Feb 2014].
Marine Accident Investigation Branch, Department of Transport. 1993. *Report of the Chief Inspector of Marine Accidents into the engine failure and subsequent grounding of the Motor Tanker Braer at Garths Ness, Shetland on 5 January 1993.* HMSO. www.maib.gov.uk/cms_resources.cfm?file=/braer-text.pdf [accessed 23 Sept 2013].
McClure, J. Derrick. 2009. *Why Scots Matters.* Edinburgh: Saltire Society.
McKeon, Belinda. 2005. 'Kathleen Jamie: Poet.' In *The Irish Times*, 15 June 2005 www.belindamckeon.com/work/kathleen-jamie-poet [accessed 27 January 2014].
Neil, Andrew. 2000. 'History in a new scheme.' In *Magma* 16 www.poetrymagazine.org.uk/magazine/notice.asp?id=291 [accessed 27 Jan 2014].
Pullman, Philip. *Grimm Tales for Young and Old.* 2012. London: Penguin.
Ross, Andrew. 1999. 'The Social Claim on Urban Ecology', interview with Michael Bennett. In *The Nature of Cities: Ecocriticism and Urban Environments.* Tucson AZ: University of Arizona Press.
Rozelle, Lee. 2006. *Ecosublime: Environmental Awe and Terror from New World to Oddworld.* Tuscaloosa: The University of Arizona Press.
Scott, Alistair, Alana Gilbert and Ayele Gelan. 2007. 'The Urban-Rural Divide: Myth or Reality.' In Socio-Economic Research Group (SERG). Aberdeen: The Maccauley Institute.
Visit.Shetland.Org The Official Site for Shetland Tourism.

CHAPTER FOUR

MAGGIE NELSON'S QUEER
MATERNAL ECOLOGY

WENDY WHELAN-STEWART

Maggie Nelson's *The Argonauts* (2015)[1], a recollection and celebration of the ever-shifting contours of Nelson's hard-earned family, is book-ended by considerations of our bleak future. Despite conundrums about how humans can "love in a time of extinction" and calls to "make kin, not babies," the book charts the author's compulsion to create a present that presupposes a future and to have a child.[2] Nelson trusts in her desire, and her memoir tells of the fruits of such trust: a sustained love affair with Harry, her lover and, later, spouse; the evolution of their individual bodies into new patterns; the bliss of Nelson's early motherhood. As an alternative to "don't reproduce and don't produce," Nelson offers up a maternal ethics that supports another as it offers space for that other's evolution.

Maggie Nelson begins *The Argonauts* with brief recollections of her love affair with Harry. The start of their romance coincides with the Santa Ana winds whipping and "shredding" California, the lovers' locale.[3] The winds serve briefly as setting for a flashback and as metaphor. As part of the "large scale patterns of atmospheric circulation," the winds are a natural feature of the earth and the California fall landscape.[4] Their existence temporarily merges with the smaller ecosystem of California. The winds are strangely, simultaneously both a common feature of California in the fall

---

[1] Nelson, Maggie, *The Argonauts*, (Minneapolis: Graywolf Press, 2015).
[2] I encountered both of these phrases by Matthew Chrulew and Donna Haraway, respectively, in the context of Eben Kirksey's "Queer Love, Gender Bending Bacteria, and Life after the Anthropocene."
[3] Nelson, 3.
[4] The U.S. Climate Change Science Program, *The Effects of Climate Change on Agriculture, Land Resources, Water Resources, and Biodiversity in the United States*, (Darby: Diane Publishing Company, 2008), 88.

and a foreign element that ravages the environment and its inhabitants—its "winds are shredding the bark off the eucalyptus trees in long white stripes".[5] Nelson calls the winds "widowmakers," but "risk[s]" them anyway to talk about her new lover with a friend. In Nelson's memoir, what savages another does so lovingly, and these winds, though briefly mentioned, are meant as a first pattern: They whip "long white stripes" from the Eucalyptus in the way we suppose Harry must do to Maggie over a romantic night she has arranged: "You took off your leather belt, smiling."[6] Both encounters seem to enact Deleuze's concept of deterritorialization, a moment when the territorial boundaries of a space are temporarily made penetrable. The result is a flourishing of growth, a bald newness.

Nelson's reconstruction of the winds' ecstatic force foretells her own romance, which involves BDSM play, but they also represent the current point of humans on a trajectory of intensifying climate changes. The dryness that the Santa Ana winds bring precludes fires that cyclically rampage wild and human-inhabited areas. With climate change producing warmer and dryer seasons for the California ecosystem, fire season will gradually dominate the calendar year.[7] It takes less than a page for Nelson to connect and juxtapose California's fraught seasonal cycle with the greenness of new love. In an early dispute between the two lovers over the merits of human language (and evolution), Nelson argues for humanism, but ends up conceding "the sadness of our eventual extinction" and, perhaps worse, "the injustice of our extinction of others.".[8] The lovers, relishing their new beginning, grapple with their world's larger demise:

> You conceded there might be an OK human, an OK human animal, even if that human animal used language, even if its use of language were somehow defining of its humanness—even if humanness itself meant trashing and torching the whole motley, precious planet, along with its, our, future.[9]

Harry throws a wrench into the usual humanist argument that elevates humans above animals because of the sophistication of human language. Language, and the humans who wield it in dominance over others, might become acceptable if humans use it relationally, to acknowledge or value their animal connections. As someone neither male nor female, Harry balks

---

[5] The U.S. Climate Change Science Program 2008, 3

[6] Nelson, *The Argonauts*, 6

[7] See Henry Fountain's Oct 28, 2019, piece in the New York Times: "How Climate Change Could Shift Santa Ana Winds, Fueling Fires."

[8] Nelson, *The Argonauts*, 4

[9] Nelson, *The Argonauts*, 6

at the colonizing force of language, "all that is unnameable falls away, gets lost, is murdered."[10] Harry begrudgingly replaces the concept of the Adamic father who names items and entities in relation to his frame of reference, his authority, with the concept of the "Ok human animal."[11]

Altered by Harry's language, Nelson adopts the use of "human animal" in other areas of *The Argonauts* and associates Harry with "the wild":

> And now, after living beside you all these years, and watching your wheel of a mind bring forth an art of pure wildness—as I labor grimly on these sentences, wondering all the while if prose is but the gravestone marking the forsaking of wildness . . . —I'm no longer sure which of us is more at home in the world, which of us more free.[12]

Harry's ability to slip out of the most rudimentary of classification systems—the gender and sex distinctions humans apply to myriad numbers of non-human organisms they share the planet with—is a sign of this wildness. Harry's graceful slip from and beyond categorization brings other humans into contact with the innately queer aspect of Nature. Nelson's attraction to and passion for Harry, she says, makes her "feral with vulnerability."[13] Rather than inhuman and disordered, feral here means essentially exposed through need and at risk of extermination or eradication. Not only does Nelson topple the hierarchy of valuations which places *feral* and *wild* low on the scale, but she also associates them with an ecocritical ethics in their fragility. (Nelson tries to cover her own naked need for Harry by writing Harry a romantic, intellectual letter, deft in its use of language and literary theory.) Harry's freedom is an echo of nature's. Animal communities (including humans) enthusiastically enjoy a wide range of sexual activities and even identities. Biologist Bruce Bagemihl (1999) in *Biological Exuberance* associates the "sexual and gender variance in animals" of the wild with "poetry."[14] "The diversity of sexuality and gender expression" becomes an occasion for "inspiring our deepest feelings of

---

[10] Nelson, *The Argonauts*, 4

[11] I take Nelson's language to be more than an indirect quote by which she might restate in her own words Harry's position. I sense that this is a kind of free indirect discourse in which the narrator's language elides with Harry's. At the conclusion of Nelson's memoir, when her memoir gives way to Harry's point of view and language, the use of *Ok* is prominent. See the very moving passages on pages 129 and 130.

[12] Nelson, *The Argonauts*, 52

[13] Nelson, *The Argonauts*, 5

[14] Bagemihl, Bruce, *Biological Exuberance: Animal Homosexuality and Natural Diversity* (New York: St. Martin's Press, 1999), 6.

wonder.".[15] There may be some of Bagemihl's sense of appreciation for this sexual exuberance in Nelson's marveling over Harry. In another instance, Nelson stands naked before Harry, who asks her to speak her unspeakable, uncontainable sexual desires into being. In this wild moment, in which the unnameable and uncategorized acts (so often found in nature) are acknowledged by the speaking, civilizing human, Harry becomes "a good animal" reacquainting a human-becoming-animal with a pre-anthropocene landscape, "an enormous mountain": "I knew you were a good animal, but felt myself to be standing before an enormous mountain, a lifetime of unwillingness to claim what I wanted, to ask for it.".[16] Nelson also mirrors Bagemihl's mysticism when she spiritualizes the history (or pre-history) of human evolution: "Our shared ancestry with earlier life forms is sacred to me.".[17]

In addition to the free-ranging queerness of Nature, the maternal is equally a wild space for Nelson. Nelson recalls an early family portrait her mother had taken of her, while visibly pregnant, with Harry and Harry's son. The image, displayed on a mug, reminds her also of a friend's criticism of the portrait as "so heteronormative" (13).[18] Trying to locate the heteronormative element, Nelson deduces that it could only have been her pregnancy that triggered the remark. Nelson asks, "How can an experience so profoundly strange and wild and transformative also symbolize or enact the ultimate conformity?"[19] Associating pregnancy with "the wild" allows us to see this state as another example of exuberant "becoming," since pregnancy wonderfully troubles Nelson's stable sense of identity and her (and anyone's) ability to control or govern other forces. Just as the eucalyptus acquiesced to the Santa Ana winds, Nelson's desire for maternity leaves her free to explore new ways of knowing or meeting a new self, herself included. Still concerned that she might be adopting a heteronormative script as she journeys into maternity, Nelson reasons that she is likely barred from a culture of queerness because femaleness is associated with predictability, and pregnancy is viewed as the ultimate act of reproducing nuclear family models. To free herself from this association, Nelson envisions herself as "the female animal," a being who lets desire lead the way. Removed from the category that sees women as men's subordinate other, woman-as-female animal also refuses to be subordinated to those truly

[15] Nelson, *The Argonauts*, 6
[16] Nelson, *The Argonauts*, 70
[17] Bagemihl, *Biological Exuberance: Animal Homosexuality and Natural Diversity*, 30
[18] Nelson, *The Argonauts*, 13
[19] Nelson, *The Argonauts*, 15

queer "nonconformi[sts]" who champion homonormativity.[20] In both of these visions of mothers, Nelson sees a tendency for the empowered to disassociate themselves from the animal kingdom in order to associate women with unaware, instinct-driven behaviors, a definition of animal that she rejects.

Again, claiming kinship with Nature while feeling the scourge of indignity during her pregnancy, Nelson criticizes Donald Winnicott, a child behaviorist she admires, for studying mothers as though they were animals while distancing himself from that category and imposing a sense of his male, human superiority. In his articles to other professionals about proper mothering, Winnicott addresses an audience of non-mothers and warns psychologists that mothers shouldn't be made aware of their tremendous impact on a child's development because they will suffer performance anxiety, "as if mothers thought they were performing their ordinary devotions in the wild, then are stunned to look up, and see a peanut-crunching crowd across a moat."[21] Winnicott refuses to participate in the awe of a person caught up in her wild, potent desire, and instead would safely demarcate it, stand comfortably and powerfully beyond the scene of mothering. Winnicott resists an opportunity to experience the mother's "becoming," a state that "moves beyond our need to know (the truth, what is real, what makes us human); beyond our determination to control (life, nature, the universe); and beyond our desire to consume/possess (pleasure, beauty, goodness, innocence)."[22]

Writing at the same time as Nelson and articulating a similar identification of newly born mothers with their sudden animal otherness is ecopoet Camille Dungy. In "After Birth," Dungy (2017b) even uses the same metaphor of the deer to represent a new mother's disassociation from her humanness. The new mothers, "common as suburban deer," realize that they have become prolific pests for their community.[23] The observation is reminiscent of Nelson's former dismissal of pregnant women as "breeders," whose bodily states make them anonymously, dismissively *"pregnant, pregnant, pregnant."*[24] Dungy's mothers-as-deer "see human faces, / human faces, human faces, all these windows," a sign that they are not only

---

[20] Nelson, *The Argonauts*, 14

[21] Nelson, *The Argonauts*, 37

[22] Sotirin, Patty, "Becoming-Woman," In *Gilles Deleuze: Key Concepts*, edited by Charles J. Stivale, (New York: Routledge, 2011), 116-117

[23] Dungy, Camille, *Guidebook to Relative Strangers: Journeys into Race, Motherhood, and History*, (New York: W. W. Norton, 2017a), 17

[24] Dungy, *Guidebook to Relative Strangers: Journeys into Race, Motherhood, and History*, 90, 91

observed by privileged non-animals from a comfortable distance, but that they are also aggressively besieged by the human for their failure to delight, since these hungry suburban deer enter "every garden [already] trampled, every feeder / emptied to spite hunger not as lovely as a birds' [sic]."[25] The neighbors have destroyed their own gardens and emptied their feeders to deprive the deer-mothers and their newborn. Just as Nelson pushes back against the attitude that the pregnant woman is simply a pawn of heteronormativity, these mothers are outside of heteronormativity, since the closed windows and gardens of the suburban neighborhood are denied them. Like Nelson, Dungy prevents readers from turning either mothers or deer into instinct-driven beasts by writing that at night, they dream of "mouths to feed and flanks to warm."[26] The concern over the limits of one's body to support the weakest and the most tender is a concern that can't be reduced to a mere instinctual motivation. Instead, the problem becomes a communal reluctance to be involved in the wildness of others' survival. In a related poem, "Trophic Cascade," Dungy (2017b) equates the mother's changing sense of self as attributable to her unspoken desires in the way wolves transformed Yellowstone's terrain through their literal hunger:

> . . . Don't
> you tell me this is not the same as my story. All this
> life born from one hungry animal, this whole,
> new landscape, the course of the river changed,
> I know this. I reintroduced myself to myself, this time
> a mother. After which, nothing was ever the same.[27]

The poem shows the magnificent growth of Yellowstone's ecosystem that comes from relocating wolves back into the park. Implied, but literally unexplained or inexplicable is the mother's storied desire that brought her into such a flourishing.

Maggie Nelson's inability to articulate her desire to mother at first seems associated with her unspeakable sexual desires. Her inability to state her sexual pleasures to her partner as she stands naked before Harry, eventually gives way to vocalizing. She exults in the sexual perversions she names. This eventual ability to speak aloud contrasts starkly with her later inability to explain that she wants a child and why: "The muteness of the desire stood

---

[25] Dungy, *Guidebook to Relative Strangers: Journeys into Race, Motherhood, and History*, 17

[26] Dungy, Camille, *Trophic Cascade*, (Middleton: Wesleyan University Press, 2017b), 18

[27] Dungy, Camille, *Trophic Cascade*, 16

in inverse proportion to its size."[28] Nelson's inability to use language marks her also as wild, animalistic, or better yet, *becoming-animal*. Nelson uses Gilles Deleuze's term, "becoming," to explain the way thwarted individuals emerge into their potential. Joao Biehl and Peter Locke (2017) make "struggle" the catalyst for "becoming," which they define as the "individual and collective struggles to come to terms with events and intolerable conditions and to shake loose, to whatever degree possible, from determinants and definitions.[29] Brent Adkins (2015), on the other side of the coin, makes "affect" the drive to "becoming": An individual is transformed by "composing himself such that certain affects were able to circulate and others were not."[30] As Nelson makes her way to biological motherhood, she bypasses obstacle after obstacle—from the passing of California's proposition 8, which recognized only heterosexual marriages and dissolved all others, to the trials of intrauterine insemination with its many disappointments and discomforts, and the fear that the semen sample is really just "egg whites."[31] Nelson's journey to maternity is mapped out by a muddling of affective states: she not only surrenders herself to the sterility of the clinic to achieve pregnancy, but she also masturbates after some of the IUI procedures, not for "romance," though the lights are dimmed and her partner holds her; not to experience her own autonomy and control, which have been lacking in the other spheres of her life; but out of a desire to get the "egg whites" as close to implanting the "bulbous" egg as possible, even knowing that the injection has already accomplished this feat.[32] Her becoming charts itself in her faltering hope, growing despair, and familiarity with weirdness. Nelson lets readers witness this weirdness, which is a dismantling of human impermeability, human precedency: An ovum has an agency that rivals Nelson's own, since it hides its readiness from Nelson (who cannot detect such a state) and from the ultrasound screen (which loses sight of it). The semen *might* be from another animal's ovary (egg whites), inviting a queer moment of Nelson's becoming-animal. A clinic's nurse implants the semen procedurally, at Nelson's request. In an earlier act that represents the wildness of queer maternity, a friend donates his semen by way of a salsa jar, allowing vegetative matter to mingle with human matter.[33]

---

[28] Nelson, *The Argonauts*, 32
[29] Deleuze, Gilles and Felix Guattari, *Anti-Oedipus: Capitalism and Schizophrenia*, (Minneapolis: University of Minnesota Press, 1983), 42
[30] Adkins, Brent, *Deleuze and Guattari's A Thousand Plateaus: A Critical Introduction and Guide.* (Edinburgh: Edinburgh University Press, 2015), 155
[31] Nelson, *The Argonauts*, 77
[32] Nelson, *The Argonauts*, 78
[33] Nelson, *The Argonauts*, 77

Again, Camille Dungy (2017a) helps inform our reading of Nelson and explains how people with a keen desire to mother an infant might slip from sensing her humanity to recognizing something of herself as belonging to the animal kingdom. For those who emphasize humankind's difference and superiority over other kinds, animal behaviors are explained by "electrical signals, hormonal imperatives . . . [n]ot emotion or reason or thought."[34] As Nelson does, Dungy troubles our easy association of human language with human exceptionalism: "Without the capacity for language, a dog or a whale or a stork is incapable of human emotion. To say a stork is sad when it loses its mate is to risk anthropomorphizing, to lose scientific objectivity, and to falsify the intellectual potential of the stork."[35] Dungy refuses to justify or engage such an argument by using its tools of dispassionate objectivity, logical reasoning, and empiricism. She uses experiences of her own affective nature to read the experiences and emotional states of communal animals: "I know the orphaned elephant wakes with nightmares, *knowing* what happened to her herd, and *mourning* that loss."[36] Dungy's knowing mirrors the elephant's "knowing:" neither argue for *how* one knows. Both elephant and Dungy are impacted by their immediate atmosphere, where each experiences her terrible existence in a place without the grounding presence of mothers, cousins, and elders. (At the moment that Dungy is thinking of the orphaned elephant, she is experiencing her daughter's first use of language and their first act of communication beyond their flesh-to-flesh communion). Dungy focuses on the body as a register for intensities and what they communicate: "This is why the caregivers of orphaned elephants sleep with the foundlings, so they do not have to wake up afraid and alone."[37] She witnesses the ways animals read or sound "the transpersonal or prepersonal intensities that emerge as bodies affect one another."[38] Dungy's own poetry is filled with sympathetic touches exchanged between mothers and babies, which her lovely line "mouths to feed and flanks to warm" represents.

---

[34] Dungy, *Guidebook to Relative Strangers: Journeys into Race, Motherhood, and History*, 17

[35] Dungy, *Guidebook to Relative Strangers: Journeys into Race, Motherhood, and History*, 17

[36] Dungy, *Guidebook to Relative Strangers: Journeys into Race, Motherhood, and History*, 17

[37] Dungy, *Guidebook to Relative Strangers: Journeys into Race, Motherhood, and History*, 17

[38] Anderson, Ben, "Affective Atmospheres." *Emotion, Space, and Society*, No. 2, 2009), 78

The image of surrogate mothers stationing themselves beside motherless elephants serves as a ready illustration of Donald Winnicott's "holding" concept, a concept applied to human and primatal relationships and one Dungy stretches in order to include other mammals. Winnicott's holding emerges from his understanding of attachment theory and "attachment figure," "the primate infant's haven of safety in times of alarm."[39] The notion of holding is essential to Nelson's *The Argonauts*, a work that depends upon the metonym of the ship that holds the Argonauts on their epic journey and is gradually reconstituted by them as the journey ruins the ship's condition and construction. Before its publication, Harry's dissatisfaction with an earlier version of the manuscript shows that it must not merely "bear adequate witness" to who Harry is and what Harry and Nelson's relationship is, but "hold" Harry and the two of them as well. Nelson's reflection on Harry's comment says as much: *". . . I do not yet understand the relationship between writing and happiness, or writing and holding."*[40] From the onset of their relationship, Nelson and Harry had been practicing the abstract, but very real act of holding Harry's young son. While Harry's estrangement from the son's mother is becoming formalized, Nelson and Harry know that they must create a literal and figurative sense of support for the toddler, who is experiencing his parents' separation. Nelson gives this safety net Donald Winnicott's term "holding," or a "consistent, empathic therapeutic environment that enables trust and growth."[41] Nelson describes the event as an emergency: "we were faced with the urgent task of setting up a home for your son that would feel abundant and containing--…rather than broken or falling."[42] In one of his favorite games with Nelson, the three-year-old pretends he "collapses" so that he can be "healed" by her, the good Blue Witch, his stepmother.[43] Holding is a repetition of the soothing environment that a mother provides her troubled infant by sound and touch, and Nelson notes that her stepson's performance of "collapsing" requires that she faithfully recite a scripted monologue of her concern and performance of healing him.[44] Successful

---

[39] Hrdy, Sarah Blaffer. *Mothers and Others: The Evolutionary Origins of Mutual Understanding,* (Cambridge: Belknap Press, 2011), 289
[40] Nelson, *The Argonauts*, 47
[41] Glasgow, Rachel, "Holding and Containing a Couple Through Periods of High Intensity: What Holds the Therapist?" (*Australian and New Zealand Journal of Family Therapy*, No. 2, 2017), 194
[42] Nelson, *The Argonauts*, 21
[43] Nelson, *The Argonauts*, 10
[44] Glasgow, "Holding and Containing a Couple Through Periods of High Intensity: What Holds the Therapist?", 201

holding requires "consistency," "empathy," "reliability," while another psychoanalytical concept, "containing," requires a mother-figure to register a child's fear, "metabolise [it]," and "feed it back" to a child in a way that is digestible.[45] Nelson *contains* her stepson when she returns her stepson's fears of abandonment and harm in the Blue Witch's monologue, "*But where could this soldier have come from? How did he get so far from home? . . . Will he be kind or fierce when he awakens? Will he know I am good...*"[46] Her first experiences mothering brings her a reciprocal sense of support as she marvels at his trust and vulnerability. She reflects with hindsight, "I understand what it is to hold the position, to be held by it."[47] In other words, she knows the difficulties of trying to parent via an unfavorably viewed role and also the incongruent reward of being supported by her stepson's participation.

The final manuscript of *The Argonauts* is Nelson's incredible answer to Harry's request that she "bear adequate witness" to their queer life. Nelson uses her experiences as a mother to fashion a responsible, jubilant response. Her book is a kind of Argo whose hull cradles and bears its family members—Harry, Harry's son (Maggie's stepson), Maggie and Harry's son, Iggy, and Maggie and Harry's mothers—bravely on. She retools the Argo as a metonymic vehicle for holding her loved ones (the Argonauts) intact and imbues the concept with a maternal ethics grounded in flux and Deleuze's "becoming" that she experienced in breastfeeding. Merging the noun's various denotations, Nelson plays on the concept of *holding*. Planks not original to the ship become part of the Argo, help brace the form that bears the name. They substitute and are renamed in a kind of metonymy, though if they are removed from the context that is the Argo, they do not retain the name. The Argo not only holds and buoys those who sail by it, but it also renames those onboard as the Argonauts. They create the ship and are created in turn. There is something of poet A.K. Ramanujan's understanding of metonymy as a context "of which a man's activities and feelings are a part. To describe the exterior landscape is to inscribe the interior landscape."[48] Ramanujan explains that the metonymic relationship of humans to their contexts is part of a system of "container-contained relations."[49] Nelson bases her sense of relationship and individuals'

---

[45] Glasgow, "Holding and Containing a Couple Through Periods of High Intensity: What Holds the Therapist?", 203
[46] Nelson, *The Argonauts*, 10
[47] Nelson, *The Argonauts*, 21
[48] Ramanujan, A. K., "Is There an Indian Way of Thinking? An Informal Essay," (*Contributions to Indian Sociology*, No. 1, 1989), 50
[49] Ramanujan, "Is There an Indian Way of Thinking? An Informal Essay," 50

responsibilities to one another in the same kind of metonymy. As an example, Nelson writes about baby Iggy: "I don't want to make the mistake of needing him as much as or more than he needs me. But there's no denying that sometimes, when we sleep together in the dark cavern of the bottom bunk . . ., Iggy's body holds mine."[50] Gestated and contained by his mother during his fetal stages and infancy, Iggy's tiny body miraculously makes his mother feel psychically intact and emotionally supported.

The Argonaut is an image of Deleuze's "becoming" phenomenon, just as it is of Winnicott's holding principle. "Becomings" are described as fluid processes. They are "pure affects," and move "above and below the threshold of perception."[51] Nelson's queering of motherhood is a contribution to maternity studies for, at the very least, giving a nursing parent the freedom to own the ecstasy of one's breastfeeding relationship with one's infant. Nelson considers Dr. Sears's reminder that a nursing mother isn't a "pedophile freak": "[T]he hormones unleashed by breast-feeding are the same as those unleashed by sex."[52] Nelson, unafraid of perversion, resists "partitioning one sexual feeling off from another, presumably more "real" sexual feeling."[53] She relies on Deleuze's vision of abundant joy: "There is in fact a joy that is immanent to desire as though desire were filled with itself and its contemplations, a joy that . . . distributes intensities of pleasures and prevents them from being suffused by anxiety, shame, and guilt."[54] Her relationship with Iggy "isn't *like* a love affair. It *is* a love affair," she asserts.[55] She performs her queering of cultural taboos with language that breaks free: "[T]he culture's worrying over pedophilia in all the wrong places at times made me feel unable to approach his genitals or anus with wonder and glee, until one day I realized, he's my baby, I can—indeed I must!—handle him freely and ably. My baby! My little butt! Now I delight in his little butt." Never has such a passage exposed the joy of dispensing with a needless taboo: there is a move from stating a philosophical criticism to voicing the warmth of pleasure. The interrupting "indeed I must!" performs the gusto of ownership in a moment when traditional maternal practices reveal unseen queer encounters. The phrase lends its exclamation mark to two other short fragments that perform joy in staccato: My baby! My little butt! There are two uses of the mommy-word "little," two uses of

---

[50] Nelson, *The Argonauts*, 45
[51] Deleuze, Gilles and Felix Guattari, *A Thousand Plateaus* (Minneapolis: University of Minnesota Press, 1987), 281
[52] Nelson, *The Argonauts*, 44
[53] Nelson, *The Argonauts*, 44
[54] Deleuze, and Guattari, *A Thousand Plateaus*, 155
[55] Nelson, *The Argonauts*, 44

the word "delight." Nelson uses ellipsis, aposiopesis (the inability to complete a statement because of emotion), and epistrophe to capture the dynamics of joy.

Right after these expressions of uncontainable joy, Nelson invokes the mundane while skillfully recalling the Argo. She writes, "I delight in pouring water over his head with a toy boat full of holes, wetting his blond curls, matted with butter from a plate he recently made into a hat" (42).[56] The Argo that initially conveyed the phrase "I love you," which must be renewed with each use," is here seen in the form of a toy boat conventionally and typically used by many an enthralled parent. The replaceable planks of the Argo are transformed into holes in the toy's hull, which safely and softly deliver just the right amount of water for a baby's fine hair and open eyes. Nelson uses consonance to link "butt" and "boat" and thereby the queer and the mundane—"My little *butt*! Now I delight in his little *butt*. I delight in pouring water . . . with a toy *boat* full of holes [emphasis added]" (42).[57] The Argonauts initially pictured in the memoir-monograph, Nelson and Harry, have become Nelson and Iggy. The reality of the first pair of lovers enables the proliferation of more pairs, all contained and contextualized by the original mutual love. This rearrangement of Argonauts, along with the water seeping through the toy boat's hull, simply conveys the theme of fluidity amid stability. The first pair will not understand their relationship until each of the partner's proliferating relationships with the other Argonauts are experienced and accounted for. This is what Nelson means by an identity as an act of "becoming." "Becoming" requires that each relationship be experienced deeply. Continuing with boat language, Nelson says simply: "I have my baby, and my baby has me. It is a buoyant eros, an eros without teleology" (44).[58] Just as the parent continues to gaze or "behold" the baby as she fills and refills and refills the holey boat with water after it has dripped itself dry, there is the accretive sense of holding, of being held. Fluidity moves freely in a hermeneutic loop, while stability always resumes after the lapse of time between the last "I love you."

Nelson embraces the concept of the sodomitical mother, a mother whose sexual pleasure cannot and will not be contained "by the dutifully instrumental" proscriptions for sexual activity as procreation.[59] Once again, Nelson elides queer mothering with the deviance and diversity of Nature. In her survey of sodomitical mothers representing themselves in art, Nelson considers A.L. Steiner's *Puppies and Babies* series, whose images of

---

[56] Nelson, *The Argonauts*, 42
[57] Nelson, *The Argonauts*, 42
[58] Nelson, *The Argonauts*, 44
[59] Nelson, *The Argonauts*, 69

absorbed or laughing mothers breastfeeding their children share spaces with images of contended, naked individuals spooning their beloved dogs. This is the excess of the sodomitical mother, one whose maternal love spills into her sexuality and sexuality spills into her doting. She speaks of Catherine Opie's "Self-Portrait/Nursing," a photographic portrait of a bare Opie momentously filling the frame while tenderly breast-feeding her equally bare son.[60] Opie's gaze is directed toward her son in a way that recalls a millennia of paintings of the Madonna Lactans, the lactating Virgin Mary. Opie's viewers see, however, that Opie is neither dutifully feminine nor dutifully procreative, and her followers know her early work with lesbian domesticity. A barely visible scar spanning above her breasts reads "Pervert," a word she etched into her flesh for an earlier portrait, "Self-Portrait/ Pervert." Opie reveals both the bloodied etching and her breasts while obscuring her face behind an SM mask. These two images present a self "becoming." In Barthes' language, the portraits are "a repertoire which is both finite and perpetual."[61] In Nelson's reading of the portrait, Opie's perversities are a "perpetual" part of her, though they are muted or "backgrounded" in early maternity. Early maternity is a finite period, but one, we are left to suppose, leaving an equally indelible mark. In both portraits Opie's excess of flesh brilliantly claims the camera eye, but only in the second portrait does the viewer feel outside of the closed loop of mutual absorption between baby and Opie. Opie demonstrates an excess that Nelson's definition of motherhood just barely grasps as the "slip[age] between gratifying another and gratifying oneself."[62]

The sudden strangeness of her own breasts during maternity takes Nelson by surprise, leaving her both disturbed and pleased. In one recollection, Nelson describes her doula as more knowing and more commanding of Nelson's body than Nelson herself is. Nelson worries that her breasts won't make milk, and the doula assures Nelson:

> *You've made it already.* Seeing me unconvinced, she said, *Want me to show you?* I nodded, shyly lifting a breast out of my bra. In one stunning gesture, she took my breast into her hand-beak and clamped down hard. A bloom of custard-colored drops rose in a ring, indifferent to my doubts.[63]

---

[60] Nelson, *The Argonauts*, 64
[61] Barthes, Roland, *Roland Barthe by Roland Barthe*. Translated by Richard Howard, (New York: Hill and Wang, 2010), 421
[62] Nelson, *The Argonauts*, 96
[63] Nelson, *The Argonauts*, 95

An embodiment of Roland Barthes' idea of the Argo, Nelson does not recognize her breasts as the ones that used to constitute her body. The breasts have altered, though Nelson (as an Argo) had *felt* herself still much the same. In a familiar and erotic act of trusting her body with a kind stranger (or a "good animal" like Harry), she witnesses its strange and wondrous capabilities. It is worth noting that Nelson's language becomes intensely figurative—"hand-beak" is metonymic in that the hand, in the shape of a baby bird's beak, represents an eventual full-bodied baby at the breast. Hand-beak also suggests that Nelson's experience of her prenatal body brings her out of her limited taxonomic rank and in closer kinship with the greater animal kingdom.

Nelson's breasts bring her new sensations, but they are recognizable, even retooled forms of previous sexual pleasures. In a paragraph that jumbles the body's changes during pregnancy and after, the syntax is intentionally fragmented. Nelson's fragmented listing of maternal parts performs a body scan of differences:

> The husky feeling in my postpartum perineum, the way my breasts filling all at once with milk is like an orgasm but more painful, powerful as a hard rain. While one nipple is getting sucked, the other sometimes sprays forth, unstoppable.[64]

The syntax here is flush with the motion of letdown: liquid *l* sounds in *filling, all, milk like* are buttressed by plosives in *postpartum perineum* and *painful, powerful*. The passage alludes to a dizzying array of metonymic couplings: Iggy, invisible but implied as the agent in the phrase "getting sucked", is here a part of the mother's pleasure, while her breast, a part of her, is momentarily his entire pleasure. There is the breastfeeding orgasm that suddenly contains the disparate parts of perineum and breasts. The final image of the one breast erupting with milk embodies the hidden processes of "pleasure" serving as "the flow of desire itself."[65] Nelson suggests that a mother in touch with her queerness can experience a trajectory beyond the point of self-knowledge: She, like other lovers, "knows no Selves because interior and exterior are equally a part of the immanence in which they have fused."[66] In these moments, blended here as one, Nelson experiences a collapsing of external and internal: She registers the autonomy of her lower ribs and the lungs making way for fetal Iggy as something a part of and beyond her; she merges with Iggy, connects even with the "dirt that collects

---

[64] Nelson, *The Argonauts*, 103
[65] Deleuze, and Guattari, *A Thousand Plateaus*, 156
[66] Nelson, *The Argonauts*, 157

on [her partem or postpartum] belly button," and realizes the way "rain" feels in a deluge as her breast sprays milk.[67] The milk is the excess of desire and the expression of immanence, or the self's ecstatic merger with humans and non-humans.

Nelson also embraces the perspective of the machine, a non-human becoming more important to generating life in the Anthropocene. Calling humans also "desiring machines," Nelson makes technology a partner in the earth's evolution.[68] In fact, she is one of the only writers to include (however ambivalently) the breast pump as a partner in infant feeding—"I estimate that about nine-tenths of the words in this book were written "free," the other one-tenth, hooked up to a hospital-grade breast pump: words piled into one machine, milk siphoned out by another."[69] Three machines are referenced in this statement: the computer (with its word processing software), the pump, and the system that includes Nelson as a component feeding material to a computer and to a pump to get an output both literal and figurative. In another moment when Nelson describes a woman's act of pumping milk, she connects the mother to both animal and machine and resists any sense of dehumanizing from the connection:

> Pumping milk is, for many women, a sharply private activity. I]t reminds the nursing mother of her animal status: just another mammal, milk being siphoned from its glands.[70]

Rather than shameful, the act is "sharply private."[71] Even the confines of gender and identity blessedly disappear as "many women" become the less specific "mammal," an "it."[72] The image of a photographed subject, who is captured while pumping and who stares into the camera without affect, stays with Nelson. She explains that the image in its muteness isn't one of "danger, suffering, illness, nihilism, or abjection."[73] It is positively charged, since the woman's milk is for another's sustenance. The attitude a mother takes while pumping may be so culturally objectionable that it isn't represented in art or literature, yet its disturbance reminds us to embrace another hidden experience of maternal queerness.

---

[67] Nelson, *The Argonauts*, 103
[68] The phrase is Deleuze's. See the chapter titled "Desiring-Machines" in *Anti-Oedipus: Capitalism and Schizophrenia (1984)*, 143
[69] Nelson, *The Argonauts*, 100
[70] Nelson, *The Argonauts*, 99
[71] Nelson, *The Argonauts*, 99
[72] Nelson, *The Argonauts*, 99
[73] Nelson, *The Argonauts*, 99

At the conclusion of the book, Nelson reflects on "endings" and resists the nihilism that dominates when humans consider their relationship to climate crisis and anticipate global extinction. Addressing her son, Nelson explains that human animals, like other animals, create more life without regard for environmental forecasts or philosophical quandaries: "two human animals, one of whom is blessedly neither male nor female, the other of whom is female (more or less), deeply, doggedly, wildly wanted you to be."[74] Rather than the nuclear family's reproduction of "more of the same," there are other evolutionary paths that queer parenting can contribute. Nelson and Harry embrace—"doggedly, wildly"—the perspectives of non-humans and their "exuberance" in living and making life. Nelson's memoir of human animals building a queer family in the Anthropocene never traffics in despair. Nelson's theorizing about maternal bodies allows her to democratically view and inhabit the experiences she shares with animals. The connection between the animal, the human and the machine is strongest in experiences of breastfeeding, which is an innately queer act, since breasts metamorphose into organs that are thoroughly strange and shocking to women and babies become lovers. Nelson's experience with the flow of both material nourishment and immaterial desire enable her to slip between the lines that divide the partial from the whole, the other from the self. As a mother who negotiates multiple fluctuations in her identity, body, and desires in concert with an-other's, Nelson learns to "hold" and "behold" Harry, her stepson, and her baby. Hers is a process that she shares with other species, who wholeheartedly adopt strange orphans and give themselves over to the joys of uncategorizable sex acts. Always orienting ourselves toward the potential of "becoming"—whether animal, machine, or other—may not be enough to keep the earth from ending. Or, it may.

Bibliography

Anderson, Ben, "Affective Atmospheres." *Emotion, Space, and Society*, No. 2, 2009), 77-81.

Adkins, Brent, *Deleuze and Guattari's A Thousand Plateaus: A Critical Introduction and Guide.* (Edinburgh: Edinburgh University Press, 2015).

Bagemihl, Bruce, *Biological Exuberance: Animal Homosexuality and Natural Diversity* (New York: St. Martin's Press, 1999).

Barthes, Roland, *Roland Barthe by Roland Barthe.* Translated by Richard Howard, (New York: Hill and Wang, 2010).

---

[74] Nelson, *The Argonauts*, 142

Biehl, Joao and Peter Locke, *Unfinished: The Anthropology of Becoming*, (Durham: Duke University Press, 2017).

Deleuze, Gilles and Felix Guattari, *Anti-Oedipus: Capitalism and Schizophrenia*, (Minneapolis: University of Minnesota Press, 1983).

Deleuze, Gilles and Felix Guattari, *A Thousand Plateaus* (Minneapolis: University of Minnesota Press, 1987).

Dungy, Camille, *Guidebook to Relative Strangers: Journeys into Race, Motherhood, and History*, (New York: W. W. Norton, 2017a).

Dungy, Camille, *Trophic Cascade*, (Middleton: Wesleyan University Press, 2017b).

Fountain, Henry, "How Climate Change Could Shift Santa Ana Winds, Fueling Fires," (*New York Times*, 28 Oct. 2019).

Glasgow, Rachel, "Holding and Containing a Couple Through Periods of High Intensity: What Holds the Therapist?" (*Australian and New Zealand Journal of Family Therapy*, No. 2, 2017), 194–210.

Hrdy, Sarah Blaffer. *Mothers and Others: The Evolutionary Origins of Mutual Understanding*, (Cambridge: Belknap Press, 2011).

Kirksey, Eben, "Queer Love, Gender Bending Bacteria, and Life after the Anthropocene," (*Theory, Culture and Society*, No. 4, 2018), 49–63.

Nelson, Maggie, *The Argonauts*, (Minneapolis: Graywolf Press, 2015).

Ramanujan, A. K., "Is There an Indian Way of Thinking? An Informal Essay," (*Contributions to Indian Sociology*, No. 1, 1989), 41–58.

Sotirin, Patty, "Becoming-Woman," In *Gilles Deleuze: Key Concepts*, edited by Charles J. Stivale, (New York: Routledge, 2011), 116-30.

The U.S. Climate Change Science Program, *The Effects of Climate Change on Agriculture, Land Resources, Water Resources, and Biodiversity in the United States*, (Darby: Diane Publishing Company, 2008).

CHAPTER FIVE

AFRICAN ECOFEMINIST ENVIRONMENTALISM IN IMBOLO MBUE'S *HOW BEAUTIFUL WE WERE*

HATICE BAY

Introduction

Europe and the US are thought to be the epistemological centers of ecocriticism and environmentalism. As Cédric Courtois argues, "Within this context of a global rise in the number of works tackling environmental issues, it is still the US and European (white, male) writers who are often, if not always, considered as having the potential to produce works that trigger (militant) action for the benefit of planet Earth."[1] In a similar vein, Chelsea Mikael Frazier points out that "In mainstream films, books, and political discourse exists the erroneous notion that Black women and their communities do not care about the natural environment, sustainability, or their own health loom large."[2] She further states that "Black feminist voices have often been seemingly absent from mainstream environmentalism and the intellectual movement that sprang forth from it in the early 1990s."[3] Even worse, despite the fact that "ecological consciousness has always been constitutive of African literature"[4] and lives, Africans are accused of passivity and ignorance when it comes to environmental issues. William Slaymaker in his essay "Ecoing the Other(s)" claims that many African

---

[1] Courtois, Cédric. "'Into the mutation:' Osahon Ize-Iyamu's 'More Sea than Tar' (2019) as Climate Fiction", *Commonwealth Essays and Studies*. 43.2. 23 July 2021. http://journals.openedition.org/ces/7510, 2.
[2] Frazier, Chelsea Mikael. "Black Feminist Ecological Thought: A Manifesto." *Atmos*. https://atmos.earth/black-feminist-ecological-thought-essay, 10.01.2020, 2020.
[3] Frazier, Chelsea Mikael. "Black Feminist Ecological Thought: A Manifesto." *Atmos*, 2020.
[4] Olaoluwa, Senayon. "There was a Time." *European Journal of English Studies*, 16:2, 2012, 125.

writers "have resisted or neglected the paradigms that inform much of global ecocriticism."[5] Likewise, Workineh Kelbessa argues that "Africans cannot be expected to make substantive contributions to the world's environmental problem and that they have no ideas or solutions to offer to many environmental issues."[6] As a response, in *Nature, Environment, and Activism in Nigerian Literature*, Sule E. Egya states, "Lettered people often regard indigenous, unlettered people as having no ecological sensibility, as having no sense of conservation and sustainability."[7] Similarly, Chika Unigwe in her *Guardian* opinion piece writes that "For years, young people across the world have been campaigning to draw attention to the crisis our planet faces, and to tackle it. Yet it seems the media is only interested in one young climate activist [Greta Thunberg]" (2019). Drawing attention to indigenous, black and brown teenage activists Unigwe opines:

> There are many more whose names we rarely, if ever, hear. Yet, frustratingly, these other activists are often referred to in the media as the "Greta Thunberg" of their country, or are said to be following in her footsteps, even in cases where they began their public activism long before she started hers – their own identities and work almost completely erased by a western media that rarely recognises progress outside its own part of the World (2019).[8]

Unigwe continues:

> This 'white savior' narrative invalidates the impact of locals working in their communities, and perpetuates the stereotype of 'the native with no agency' who cannot help themselves. As an African I find these portrayals deeply offensive. It is insulting to present the members of the communities most threatened by climate change as passive onlookers who are only now being spurred on by the 'Thunberg effect' (2019).[9]

---

[5] Slaymaker, William. "Ecoing the Other(s): The call of global green and black African responses." *PMLA* 116(1): 2001, 132.
[6] Kelbessa, Workineh. 'The rehabilitation of Indigenous Environmental Ethics in Africa'. *Diogenes*, 207: 2006, 21.
[7] Egya, Sule E. *Nature, Environment, and Activism in Nigerian Literature*. London and New York: Routledge, 2020, 25.
[8] Unigwe, Chika. "It's Not Just Greta Thunberg: Why Are We Ignoring the Developing World's InspiringActivists?" *The Guardian*,
https://www.theguardian.com/commentisfree/2019/oct/05/greta-thunberg-developing-world-activists. 5 October 2019.
[9] Unigwe, Chika. "It's Not Just Greta Thunberg: Why Are We Ignoring the Developing World's InspiringActivists?" *TheGuardian*.

As these scholars indicate, African environmental issues, African environmental leadership, and Africa-focused ecocriticism have not received the attention they deserve. In this article, I will explore how Mbue's novel shows that African literary landscape and ordinary African people, especially women, have never expressed "ecohesitation"[10] but love of nature, ecological agency and environmental activism. To highlight the way Mbue raises awareness against different forms of environmental being, destruction, struggles and promise of an Africa(n)-focused ecocriticism, I approach Mbue's text through African ecofeminism that is founded on African communitarian philosophy and *ubuntu*.[11]

HBWW as an African Ecofeminist Environmentalist Novel

HBWW tells the story of Kosawa, a fictional village in Africa and its invasion by an American oil company Pexton. The town and its inhabitants used to live harmoniously with nature before their fatal encounter with European and American patriarchal capitalists. The title of the novel, *How Beautiful We Were,* also suggests a bygone existence of pristine nature and blissful community. Since the precolonial times in Kosawa, humans and nonhumans have always been together and fared together. In fact, the villagers believe in a legend that says they carry the blood of a she-leopard:

> Every child in Kosawa knows about how three brothers once went to check on their traps in the forest and found a leopard caught in one of them. Please, free me, the leopard cried to the brothers; I need to return home to my children, I've been in this trap for days and they have no one to protect them […] Ultimately, the brothers decided to let her go home to her children. In gratitude, the leopard made a cut on her paw and asked the brothers to use their spears and make cuts on their fingers too. On this day, the leopard said she forged a blood pact with each brother, I give you my blood: it will flow in your veins and the veins of your descendants until the sun ceases to rise.[12]

This legend conveys the essence of the Kosawans: animals are active agents in constructing this African human community. Kosawans repeatedly

[10] Slaymaker, William. "Ecoing the Other(s): The call of global green and black African responses." *PMLA* 116(1): 2001, 132

[11] Chemhuru, Munamato. "Interpreting Ecofeminist Environmentalism in African Communitarian Philosophy and *Ubuntu*: An Alternative to Anthropocentrism." *Philosophical Papers*, 2018.

[12] Mbue, Imbolo. *How Beautiful We Were.* New York: Random House, 2021, 30-31.

remind themselves that they "carry the blood of the leopard"[13] and they are *"[s]ons of the leopard, daughters of the leopard"* (italics in the original).[14] In addition to their belief in being the descendants of a leopard, they believe that their land is sacred because their human ancestors lived on it beforehand and passed it down on them. In addition, they believe in the Spirit which is in their midst and guides and protects them.[15]

The Spirit, the land, rivers, animals, and air are so ingrained and intertwined with this community that their language, the way they see the world, and how they express themselves reflect this. Nature proverbs, metaphors and anthropomorphism are copiously interspersed within the narrative: "Papa is the only one I ever truly yearn to talk to, because our conversations were like the rustling of leaves, slow and gentle, followed by silence"[16]; "the twins were palm nuts that could never be cracked open";[17] our fathers joked about how the Pexton captives shrunk Woja Beki "from a leopard to a rabbit"[18]; and Thula was "a dove forging through a fire, burning yet soaring."[19] Evidently, the novel highlights "the interconnectedness of all life, between the human and the nonhuman realms, on the one hand, and the human and the ancestral and spirit realms, on the other."[20] The African ecofeminist implication of this also becomes obvious: contrary to European and American expansionists and anthropocentric mindset, this African community is driven by various elements of nature which, along with the human world, strive for a non-subjugationist and fruitful co-existence. Ikuenobe remarks that "[t]raditional African thought sees nature as holistic and as an interconnected continuum of humans and all natural objects which exist in harmony."[21] He goes on to write that, "There is no conceptual or ontological gap between human activities and supernatural activities of God, gods, spirits, ancestors in African thought; they are interrelated and one is an extension of the other."[22] This view reflects the African philosophy of *ubuntu*, which according to Chemhuru has ecofeminist overtones. An

---

[13] Mbue, Imbolo. *How Beautiful We Were*, 191.
[14] Mbue, Imbolo. *How Beautiful We Were*, 31.
[15] Mbue, Imbolo. *How Beautiful We Were*, 9.
[16] Mbue, Imbolo. *How Beautiful We Were*, 56.
[17] Mbue, Imbolo. *How Beautiful We Were*, 85.
[18] Mbue, Imbolo. *How Beautiful We Were*, 121.
[19] Mbue, Imbolo. *How Beautiful We Were*, 320.
[20] Kwenda, Chirevo V. "Affliction and Healing: Salvation in African Religion." *Journal of Theology in Southern Africa*, 103, 1999, 10.
[21] Ikuenobe, Polycarp A. "Traditional African Environmental Ethics and Colonial Legacy." International Journal of Philosophy and Theology, Vol. 2, No. 4, 2014, 2.
[22] Ikuenobe, Polycarp A. "Traditional African Environmental Ethics and Colonial Legacy," 5.

essential feature of *ubuntu* is that "a good human being is one who treats both human and non-human beings (nature included) in a humane way."[23] Chemhuru explains that *ubuntu* "[seeks] to emphasise the need to treat various aspects of nature that have traditionally been considered as morally insignificant—such as non-human animate beings—with care, reverence, kindness and accord them ethical consideration."[24] For instance, Thula and her father wonder "if stalks of grass live in fear of the day they'd be trampled upon."[25] This attitude reflects *ubuntu* because "it entails being considerate, kind, magnanimous and compassionate to various aspects of nature that possess life and some of which are sentient just like human beings themselves."[26]

Moreover, communitarian existence is ecofeminist per se as Chemhuru argues. In other words, breaking the male-dominated system and offering a more-than-human based community that is shaped by spirits, animals, ancestors, and nature, is ecofeminist. In the novel, it is the communal duty of every member of the community to save, protect, and defend mother nature. Many men lost their lives for their children and posterity because they wanted them to "grow up in clean Kosawa."[27] Thula affirms this viewpoint saying: "Yes, if we are to be conquered, let it not be because we never fought. Our fathers, brothers, uncles, friends-what did they die for? They died so that we could live peacefully in Kosawa, and if not us, then at least the next generation."[28] At the same time, Kosawans reflect the philosophy of *ubuntu* which is also about "a moral obligation towards others including past, present and future generations. In this way it advocates for a sustainable life that does not affect the ability of others, including future generations, to live."[29] In summary, the African brand of ecofeminism includes an emphasis on nature over culture; the centrality of posterity, cooperation, communal existence, and "the ethics of love, care, respect and

---

[23] Chemhuru, Munamato. "Interpreting Ecofeminist Environmentalism in African Communitarian Philosophy and *Ubuntu*: An Alternative to Anthropocentrism." *Philosophical Papers*, 2018, 17.

[24] Chemhuru, Munamato. "Interpreting Ecofeminist Environmentalism in African Communitarian Philosophy and *Ubuntu*: An Alternative to Anthropocentrism," 20.

[25] Mbue, Imbolo. *How Beautiful We Were,* 30.

[26] Chemhuru, Munamato. "Interpreting Ecofeminist Environmentalism in African Communitarian Philosophy and *Ubuntu*: An Alternative to Anthropocentrism," 17.

[27] Mbue, Imbolo. *How Beautiful We Were,* 86.

[28] Mbue, Imbolo. *How Beautiful We Were,* 213.

[29] Cooper, Emily." How can the African philosophy of ubuntu help change the way we think about climate change in the West?"
https://www.sheffield.ac.uk/geography/news/how-canafrican-philosophy-ubuntu-help-change-way-we-think-about-climate-change-west.

responsibility, all of which could inform non-anthropocentric environmental ethics."[30]

However, the general fecundity of Kosawa and the peaceful existence of human and more-than-human entities are destroyed by the extractive activities of an American oil company Pexton. The story starts in 1980 and goes over forty years. But in 1980, the village had already been contaminated for many years by Pexton. The first sentences of the novel set the environmental tone of the novel: "We should have known the end was near. How could we not have known? When the sky began to pour acid and rivers began to turn green, we should have known our land would soon be dead."[31] "We hated that we went to bed in fear and woke up in fear, all day long breathed fear in and out,"[32] the villager's lament. Thula continues to tell:

> Within a year, fishermen broke down their canoes and found new uses for the wood. Children began to forget the taste of fish. The smell of Kosawa became the smell of crude. The noise from the oil field multiplied; day and night we heard it in our bedrooms, in our classrooms, in the forest. Our air turned heavy.[33]

The environmental disaster Pexton caused affects mostly children: "our siblings and cousins and friends [...] had perished from the poison in the water and the poison in the air and the poisoned food growing from the land."[34] Thus, the conversation of the Kosawans revolves around environmental destruction: "Countless were the hours when we spoke of little else but Pexton."[35] These quotations describe the extent of the pollution that has impacted the minds and bodies of Kosawans. Their lived environment and their whole beings have become the dumpsite of American patriarchal waste. As an African ecofeminist text, Mbue's novel frames the American oil company largely responsible for this pollution as the manifestation of male dominance and profiteering.

The profit-driven company systematically tries to remove agency and dignity from the Kosawans but they are not willing to accept their fate. They declare that "it was our land, come rainy season or dry season, it would

---

[30] Chemhuru, Munamato. "Interpreting Ecofeminist Environmentalism in African Communitarian Philosophy and *Ubuntu*: An Alternative to Anthropocentrism." *Philosophical Papers*, 2018, 6.

[31] Mbue, Imbolo. *How Beautiful We Were*, 3.

[32] Mbue, Imbolo. *How Beautiful We Were*, 8-9.

[33] Mbue, Imbolo. *How Beautiful We Were*, 32.

[34] Mbue, Imbolo. *How Beautiful We Were*, 5.

[35] Mbue, Imbolo. *How Beautiful We Were*, 292.

always be ours."[36] In order to claim their lands, the representatives of the village go to Bézam, the operational headquarters of Pexton, to draw attention to the environmental degradation and child-death they have caused. They are ready to do anything to restore and reclaim their land, water, and air. Bongo says:

> we're not beggars, but we'll travel to Bézam and lie prostrate before these men, kiss their feet no matter how dusty their shoes, because we need their help if we're to grow old on our land. We'll make several trips to Bézam if need be; we'll continue travelling and pleading and gifting until we succeed in bringing at least one big man from the government and one powerful man from Pexton to Kosawa[…][We]'ll lay our sick children at their feet, beg them to protect these helpless ones. We may be proud, but our pain has abased us, and we will do this and more for the sake of our descendants.[37]

And yet most men who defend their environment inexplicably disappear or are massacred. Mbue illustrates how the death of men and children because of the pollution engenders the misery of women and affects them the worst. They bear the brunt of the environmental disasters caused by Pexton because they become childless and husbandless all at once. Juba says that after his father's disappearance he has "a burdened mother, an oft-distant sister, a broken grandmother."[38] His mother Sahel, after losing her husband Malabo, complains that she is doomed to "a life of being solely responsible for a broken girl and a lost boy and an old woman, all of them laying upon my back their anger and grief, with no one to bear mine but me, because it had to be so."[39] The predicament of women and that of land is entwined, as this African ecofeminist narrative depicts. As such, the women and children become the most victimized in the schemes masterminded by the foreign male establishment. Mbue shows in Chemhuru's words that the ecofeminist view has to "[challenge] humanity to consider the environment as a serious feminist issue."[40]

Kosawans get dejected and get hopeless, but then they pick up and carry on. They continue to try to reach out to Pexton representatives and speak out their demands and worries. However, Mbue begs us to question the efficacy of negotiation, dialogue and patience, and a US-based human rights

---

[36] Mbue, Imbolo. *How Beautiful We Were,* 196.
[37] Mbue, Imbolo. *How Beautiful We Were,* 89.
[38] Mbue, Imbolo. *How Beautiful We Were,* 327.
[39] Mbue, Imbolo. *How Beautiful We Were,* 150.
[40] Chemhuru, Munamato. "Interpreting Ecofeminist Environmentalism in African Communitarian Philosophy and *Ubuntu*: An Alternative to Anthropocentrism." *Philosophical Papers*, 2018, 12.

organization because all these factors have not worked in the case of this African community: "Despite comporting ourselves for decades, despite never resorting to beastly deeds, we hadn't succeeded in persuading our tormentors that we were people deserving of the privilege of living our lives as we wished."[41] Irresponsible and intransigent, Pexton remains unconcerned about its involvement in contaminating Kosawa. The villagers, therefore, resort to violence after they have failed to have their demands met through complaints, speaking, and waiting. They burn Pexton buildings, damage the pipelines, set fires, and destroy their tanks in order to let Pexton know that they are there and they are angry.[42] They rationalize:

> Yes, if we are to be conquered, let it not be because we never fought. Our fathers, brothers, uncles, friends-what did they die for? [...] No one has the right to make us prisoners on our land. No one has the right to take from us that which the Spirit gave our ancestors [...] [W]e're not weak, a ferocious creature gave us its blood. The government and Pexton have left us with no choice but to do what we must in order to be heard. They speak to us in the language of destruction- let's speak it to them too, since it's what they understand.[43]

Although they merely want to instill fear in Pexton and show that they would stop at nothing, their efforts do not pay off—in fact, they worsen everything. The government gets tougher on lawbreakers and more and more Kosawans get killed. Neither their efforts of negotiation, dialogue, peaceful protests, dancing, nor their vigilantism helps Pexton pack up and leave. Mbue looks at the unique challenges that people face when they try to lead a movement or rightfully defend their lands. In this premise, *HBWW* shows that, in practice, eco-activism may not turn out to be as planned or intended because "the world operated under laws [we] could not change."[44] However, making the headlines in some US newspapers by breaking the story about Pexton's misdeeds and voicing their dire condition are powerful strategies of resistance on the Kosawans' part.

The female protagonist Thula embarks on a life-long battle against Pexton to rescue the ecosystem from further destruction. The inexplicable disappearance of her father, the brutal way her uncle is hanged, and neighbors are gunned down, are tragic events that pave the way for Thula's activism. At the age of ten, she promises herself that she will make Woja

---

[41] Mbue, Imbolo. *How Beautiful We Were,* 188.
[42] Mbue, Imbolo. *How Beautiful We Were,* 212.
[43] Mbue, Imbolo. *How Beautiful We Were,* 213-214.
[44] Mbue, Imbolo. *How Beautiful We Were,* 338.

Beki and his friends in Bézam pay for what they have done to her family.[45] She says, "I promised myself after the massacre that I would acquire knowledge and turn it into a machete that would destroy all those who treat us like vermin,"[46] she adds. She is so determined that she reads *Pedagogy of the Oppressed, The Wretched of the Earth, The Communist Manifesto* [47] and goes to the US in order to get higher education and rise against the capitalist and patriarchal powers like Pexton. Through education, she becomes an adamant dissident who can lead a protest and rally people against Pexton.

After she returns from the US, Thula is keen to practice what she has read, seen, and learned. Shockingly, she sees that it is not only Pexton but mostly the corrupt leader of the country that stands in the way of their holistic and organic way of life where humans are constitutive of and constituted by nature. Mbue shows that Kosawans and their land are jointly subjugated by two patriarchic powers, Pexton and His Excellency, the military dictator of the country, at the same time. All along, it has been their own political leader that supported Pexton and exacerbated the problem.

The Kosawans have witnessed that, "Pexton wanted more of our oil. Our government wanted more of their money. His Excellency wanted more of the world's finest things."[48] However, the villagers who only possess machetes, spears, stones and pots of boiling water[49] cannot keep up their fight against machine guns and soldiers. The presence of a military dictatorship and lack of resources in this imaginary African country makes movements or activism almost impossible. Evidently, sustainable activism needs a democratic baseline. In order to confront the environmental crisis that has engulfed her village, Thula sees the urgent need to address various social and political issues of her country. Therefore, she travels from town to town, organizes massive nationwide protests, and raises locals' awareness against the exploits of the leaders. In front of a crowd, she advocates for people-driven power and a bottom-up approach to change:

> 'Power to the people,' she cried with her fists clenched up.
> 'Power to the people,' the crowd cried back.
> ...
> 'This land is our land.' Roars.
> 'We'll take it back whether they like it or not.' Roars.

---

[45] Mbue, Imbolo. *How Beautiful We Were,* 48.
[46] Mbue, Imbolo. *How Beautiful We Were,* 208.
[47] Mbue, Imbolo. *How Beautiful We Were,* 164.
[48] Mbue, Imbolo. *How Beautiful We Were,* 137.
[49] Mbue, Imbolo. *How Beautiful We Were,* 22.

'We'll no longer be slaughtered, poisoned, or trampled upon.' Roars. 'Let those who stand in the way of our peace and happiness be warned. Let them know that we'll march through the streets of Lojunka and district capitals around the country. We'll clench our fists until we get to Bézam. We'll roar until they give us back our dignity. Our voices will be the fire that will burn down every system of injustice, and from the ashes we will build a new nation.'[50]

Thula's eco-activism aims to dismantle the militaristic patriarchy and the subsequent enthronement of a democratic society and civilian life. She knows that her ideals are far-fetched; yet "that was no deterrent to her, only a motivation to continue the work the past generation had started so that future generations might complete it and never stop building upon it."[51] Obviously, in African ecofeminism, eco-activism is not only limited to the defense of the environment. African ecofeminism is inseparable from social and political injustices. Era Kraja affirms this by writing that "eco-activism is not just about ecology: it's also one of the best ways to bring about social and political change."[52] As Chemhuru also states "the African ecofeminist philosophical view, which challenges all forms of domination and oppression, implies that if the origin of human social and political problems is understood and addressed, then it would also be easier to comprehend and address environmental problems as well."[53] Thula, at least, achieves to mobilize locals against their own politicians who by legitimizing Pexton's presence are foremost responsible for the degradation of their environment and their dire condition. African ecoactivism, therefore, becomes the quest for democracy, freedom of expression, gaining ownership of one's own lives, and fairness.

Conclusion

Mbue's narrative sets out to expand the scope of the rather US/European-dominated ecoactivism and ecocriticism. Mbue presents an environmentally sensitive novel that highlights the roles the African teenagers, community and women play in fighting petrodollar capitalists. The way the villagers lay their lives for the sake of their ancestors, environment, and future generations attests to the fact that African people are ecologically conscious and are not

---

[50] Mbue, Imbolo. *How Beautiful We Were,* 312.-313.
[51] Mbue, Imbolo. *How Beautiful We Were,* 296.
[52] Kraja, Era. "Eco-activism: what it is and why it is relevant." https://www.wecf.org/eco-activism-what-it-is-and-why-it-is-relevant/, 13. April 2018.
[53] Mbue, Imbolo. *How Beautiful We Were,* 10.

passive spectators in the face of environmentally destructive forces. African people's defense for their environment involves fighting against the local capitalists and the dictatorial regime as well. Thus, African ecofeminism encompasses pro-democratic activities. Finally, *HBWW* demonstrates that indigenous African communities that live a communitarian life and are guided by *ubuntu,* are exemplary with regard to environmental issues, i.e. consciousness, conservation, relationship, defense and therefore, enrich ecocritical thinking. Although Thula's and the Kosawans' ecoactivism resulted largely in defeat, in the future their meaningful fight and struggle will impact their more-than-human community and posterity in a positive way.

Bibliography

Chemhuru, Munamato. "Interpreting Ecofeminist Environmentalism in African Communitarian Philosophy and *Ubuntu*: An Alternative to Anthropocentrism." *Philosophical Papers*, 2018, pp. 1- 24.

Cooper, Emily." How can the African philosophy of ubuntu help change the way we think about climate change in the West?" https://www.sheffield.ac.uk/geography/news/how-canafrican-philosophy-ubuntu-help-change-way-we-think-about-climate-change-west.

Courtois, Cédric. "'Into the mutation:' Osahon Ize-Iyamu's 'More Sea than Tar' (2019) as Climate   Fiction", *Commonwealth Essays and Studies*. 43.2. 23 July 2021. http://journals.openedition.org/ces/7510.

Egya, Sule E. *Nature, Environment, and Activism in Nigerian Literature.* London and New York: Routledge, 2020.

Frazier, Chelsea Mikael. "Black Feminist Ecological Thought: A Manifesto." *Atmos.* https://atmos.earth/black-feminist-ecological-thought-essay, 10.01.2020.

Ikuenobe, Polycarp A. "Traditional African Environmental Ethics and Colonial Legacy." International Journal of Philosophy and Theology, Vol. 2, No. 4, 2014, pp. 1-21.

Kelbessa, Workineh. 'The rehabilitation of Indigenous Environmental Ethics in Africa'. *Diogenes*, 207: 2006, pp. 17-34.

Kraja, Era. "Eco-activism: what it is and why it is relevant." https://www.wecf.org/eco-activism-what-it-is-and-why-it-is-relevant/, 13. April 2018.

Kwenda, Chirevo V. "Affliction and Healing: Salvation in African Religion." *Journal of Theology in Southern Africa*, 103, 1999, pp. 1–12.

Mbue, Imbolo. *How Beautiful We Were.* New York: Random House, 2021.

Moolla, F. Fiona. "Introduction." *Natures of Africa: Ecocriticism and Animal Studies in Contemporary Cultural Forms.* Edited by F. Fiona Moolla, Wits University Press, 2016, pp. 1–26.

Olaoluwa, Senayon. "There was a Time." *European Journal of English Studies*, 16:2, 2012, pp. 125-136.

Slaymaker, William. "Ecoing the Other(s): The call of global green and black African responses." *PMLA* 116(1): 2001, pp. 129-144.

Unigwe, Chika. "It's Not Just Greta Thunberg: Why Are We Ignoring the Developing World's Inspiring Activists?" *The Guardian*, https://www.theguardian.com/commentisfree/2019/oct/05/greta-thunberg-developing-world-activists. 5 October 2019.

CHAPTER SIX

NATURE AND INDIAN SENSIBILITY: AN ECOCRITICAL READING OF SAROJINI NAIDU'S SELECT POEMS

SHUBHANKU KOCHAR

It is now a commonly held view that before the advent of Western ideas of development and progress, inflicted through the expansion of colonies and the empire, highly evolved and literate societies in India had already given emphasis to an environmentally balanced way of life wherein nature was sacralised and worshipped.[1]

Sarojini Naidu, a representative poet of her times whose poetry is living example of this belief, is hailed as the "Nightingale of India" and "one of the greatest Indian English-poetess." She wrote poetry in which she described the beauty of the Indian landscape, about the Hindu-Muslim unity, about the common man and woman, and about the culture of India. Her poems are easy to read, easy to recite and very easy to remember because of their inherent musicality. As a result, her appeal is beyond cultures and nationalities. When one reads Sarojini's poetry, the first idea that usually strikes the readers is her exquisite and fine delicacy of feelings and expressions combined with freshness and exuberance of spirit. Some of her notable works are: "The Festival of Memory," "Palanquin Bearers," "To a Buddha seated on a Lotus," "Wandering Singers," and "Guerdon." She inundates her poems with the vital rhythms of the universe. Naidu has artistically captured almost all the sides of the richly coloured Indian life that throbs around her. In her poetry, Naidu delineates not only the soft aspects of nature, but also the terrific and cruel features, such as, volcanic

---

[1] Sivaramakrishnan, Murali, "Ecopoetics and the Literature of Ancient India". In *A Global History of Literature and the Environment,* edited by John Parham and Louise Westling, (Cambridge: Cambridge UP, 2016), 66

eruptions, stormy winds and tempestuous oceans. Nature to her is what it was to Tennyson "an inevitable and alive background for the portrayal of human emotions."[2] The present chapter aims to argue the following with reference to the poems by Sarojini Naidu: How Naidu represents Indian sensibility towards nature in her poetry. What are various patterns visible in Naidu's representation of nature? What is the relevance of Naidu's poetry from an ecocritical perspective today after almost hundred years of its publication?

Arthur Symons recalls in his Introduction to, *The Golden Threshold,* that Naidu expressed poetically herself in one of her letters, "'but I sing just as the birds do, and my songs are as ephemeral' It is for this bird-like quality of song, it seems to me, that they are to be valued."[3] Naidu makes passing references to nature in her poems. It is not difficult to come across trees, rivers, flowers, forests, birds and animals in her poems. Her similes and metaphors are usually drawn from nature. It seems that her protagonists look around and pick references from natural surroundings. Consider these famous lines from "Palanquin Bearers:"

> 'Lightly, O lightly we bear her along,
> She sways like a flower in the wind of our song;
> She skims like a bird on the foam of a stream.'[4]

Likewise, these lines from "Wandering Singers" can also be cited (written to one of their tunes):

> 'Where the voice of the wind calls our wandering feet,
> Through echoing forest and echoing street,
> With lutes in our hands ever-singing we roam.'[5]

Similarly, in "Indian Weavers," the speaker gets the following reply when he inquires that why the weavers weave what they weave:

> Weavers, weaving at fall of night,
> Why do you weave a garment so bright?
> Like the plumes of a peacock, purple and green,
> We weave the marriage-veils of a queen.[6]

---

[2] Naidu, Sarojini and Symons, Arthur, *The Golden Threshold: With an Introduction by Arthur Symons,* (London: William Heinemann, 1905).
[3] Naidu, *The Golden Threshold,* 1
[4] Naidu, *The Golden Threshold,* 5
[5] Naidu, *The Golden Threshold,* 2
[6] Naidu, *The Golden Threshold,* 3

These examples show that Naidu is very conscious about her surroundings. There is smoothness and elegance in her diction and form which takes shapes from nature. Her poems are rooted in natural landscapes and her speakers are men and women of soil. Her characters are in sync with nature around them. Overtly, she does not talk about natural disasters, because the time that shaped and coloured her perspective did not witness eco-hazards, at least from an Indian perspective, but nevertheless, nature emerges as a prominent force in her poetry. It indicates that Indian consciousness is incomplete without reference to nature.

Arthur Symons quotes yet another letter of Naidu in his Introduction that gives a peep into her psyche as a lover of nature. He records:

> Come and share my exquisite March morning with me: this sumptuous blaze of gold and sapphire sky; these scarlet lilies that adorn the sunshine; the voluptuous scents of neem and champak and Sirisha that beat upon the languid air with their implacable sweetness; the thousand-little gold and blue and silver breasted birds bursting with the shrill ecstasy of life in nesting time. All is hot and fierce and passionate, ardent and unashamed in its exulting and importunate desire for life.[7]

As Fisher articulates, Indian sensibility has retained a sense of gratitude towards nature. Indians have been worshiping her since antiquity. In the Indian context, nature is hailed as mother.

Indians have been educated since eternity to respect and venerate her as a Goddess. Indian children are brought up with a sense of value towards nature and human-beings. They are taught to water plants daily. They are made to memorize the hymns related to sun, moon, rain, sky, and the earth, herself. They are taught the lesson to the Earth being home of everyone including the human and nonhuman. They are supposed to offer water to the sun and moon daily in traditional households. They learn from their parents to offer food and water to birds and animals.

Naidu in, "Coromandel Fishers," demonstrates such an ideology through her protagonist. Her speaker is a fisherman. When the poem begins it is dawn and the protagonist is motivating his fellows to get up and be ready for the day's work. He urges his folks to hurry otherwise it will be late. He tells them that they should remain courteous towards the Sea as they get their sustenance from the Water. He encourages them to express their gratitude to the forces of nature that sustain them. He reminds them:

---

[7] Naidu, *The Golden Threshold*, 5

"The sea is our mother,
the cloud is our brother,
the waves are our comrades."[8]

Naidu also captures the voices of birds and animals. Her sensitivity is comprehensive enough to present culturally muted voices. She makes her readers conscious of their unjust actions. In her poems, she sympathises with these beautiful creatures. For example, in "Corn-Grinders," she unfolds the senseless killing of rats and deer. In presenting the plight of these animals, she boldly comments on the selfish and ego-centric nature of man.

In the poem quoted above, Naidu ridicules mankind for exercising power without prudence. The speaker in this poem encounters first a small rat who is weeping. On being asked, the rat informs the speaker that her mate has been killed by the rich farmer when the former was trying to get little food for himself and his family. One feels sympathy with the female rat since everyone has the right to exist and survive. When one kills a tiny creature like a rat, one destroys an ecosystem. There are things that a rat can do, and he does them without failing. Rats are one of the longest surviving species on the face of this Earth. They sustained when even the dinosaurs perished. They impart this wonderful wisdom of adapting oneself with humility in adverse circumstances. The loss of one rat, in this context, is the loss of one teacher. This is how Naidu paints the scene:

Alas! alas! my lord is dead!
Ah, who will ease my bitter pain?
He went to seek a millet-grain
In the rich farmer's granary shed;
They caught him in a baited snare,
And slew my lover unaware.[9]

In the same poem, Naidu also mocks the senseless slaughter of deer by hunters. Deer have been long hunted for musk. They have also been slaughtered for food. Here also, Naidu presents a painful picture of a deer who has lost his mate. As Barry Commoner argues that everything is connected to everything else in nature, it goes without saying that when one participant is removed from the food chain, it disrupts the entire chain. For example, deer eat grass, it keeps the grass from over growing, deer are also eaten by animals like lions and leopards. If deer are removed from this

---

[8] Naidu, *The Golden Threshold*, 4
[9] Naidu, *The Golden Threshold*, 5

chain, grass grows into thickets and animals who are dependent upon deer for their food, start to die. It disturbs the entire ecosystem.

Naidu delivers such a jam of eco-wisdom that if followed can certainly enrich human experience on this Earth. Here also, one feels bad for the deer who has lost her mate. Naidu paints a vivid picture of the grieving deer:

> Alas! alas! my lord is dead!
> Ah! who will quiet my lament?
> At fall of eventide, he went
> To drink beside the river-head;
> a waiting hunter threw his dart,
> And struck my lover through the heart.[10]

In "Village Song," Naidu delves upon the mischievous nature of human society. She presents the contrast between nature and culture. Her argument is that the human world is full of sorrows, whereas the natural world is inundated with joy, happiness and bliss. She presents a mother who is pleading with her daughter to stay back. Her daughter is inclined towards leaving human society, as she argues that the forest is full of comfort and joy. She says that she is being called by the fairies. Her mother tries to convince her with mouth-watering descriptions of the world. She informs her that her wedding is approaching, and she will get colourful clothes and her husband will come leading a mighty procession.

The daughter rejects all this as futile. She tells her mother that human society is full of suffering and troubles. She regards this world as an illusion and declares that she would prefer to stay in a forest where there is happiness and gaiety. This is how she counters her mother:

> Mother mine, to the wild forest I am going,
> Where upon the champa boughs the champa
> buds are blowing;
> To the koil-haunted river-isles where lotus lilies glisten,
> The voices of the fairy folk are calling me:
> O listen![11]

This attitude continues throughout the poem. The mother keeps on persuading and the daughter keeps on refuting. This wisdom is surely required today if one wants to save our planet. People in their absolute greed are disturbing the flow of nature. They are madly running after material goods. For them, society matters more than anything. This poem certainly

---

[10] Naidu, *The Golden Threshold*, 5
[11] Naidu, *The Golden Threshold*, 11

reminds the reader of the illusory nature of the world in comparison to the
natural world which is everlasting and fulfilling. The answer given by the
daughter can become a chant and can certainly salvage this planet if taken
seriously and repeated regularly:

> The bridal-songs and cradle-songs have cadences of sorrow,
> The laughter of the sun to-day,
> the wind of death to-morrow.
> Far sweeter sound the forest-notes where forest- streams are falling;
> O mother mine, I cannot stay,
> the fairy-folk are calling.[12]

Today, everyone wants factory made products. One finds no time to
explore natural things. In this fast-paced world, everyone is busy. It is easy
to procure things in a supermarket today. One can place an order from the
comfort of home by clicking one button. Even fruits, vegetables and milk
are bought and sold in the supermarkets. These products are presented in
such a manner that one feels like buying them without any logic. They are
packed in glittering covers and arranged aesthetically. Natural products like
milk, fruits, vegetables and flowers are presented in such a manner that they
do not betray any association with the natural world from where they come
from.

"In Praise of Henna," Naidu takes her readers to the heart of a garden
where young girls are gathering henna leaves. They are busy squeezing
henna drops so that they can utilize it for their day-to-day needs. These girls
are conscious of the benefits of this particular plant and they are likely to
respect the final product because they have themselves made it. One can
feel their enthusiasm in the following lines:

> Hasten, maidens, hasten away
> To gather the leaves of the henna-tree.
> Send your pitchers afloat on the tide,
> Gather the leaves ere the dawn be old,
> Grind them in mortars of amber and gold,
> The fresh green leaves of the henna-tree.[13]

Indian society, as Sivaramakrishnan maintains, traditionally has been
dominated by agriculture. People have been farming for ages. Before the
arrival of Europeans, the Indian worldview was animist and holistic. People
associated forces of nature with divinity. They used to live in harmony with

---

[12] Naidu, *The Golden Threshold*, 14
[13] Naidu, *The Golden Threshold*, 15

their surroundings. They used to pray to the sun god, moon god, wind, water, fire and earth. According to ancient texts of Hindu scriptures, people used to thank and revere everything around them. As Michael Fisher also remarks that in ancient India, people used to thank the God of agriculture before planting and harvesting. In "Harvest Hymn," Naidu presents such a society that believes in humility and gratitude.

She presents people worshiping nature and thanking her for her benediction. They are praying to the God of harvest and acknowledging his supremacy. They are also praying to the God of ox and plough that shows their pattern of coexistence and symbiosis. They bow their heads in utter modesty before the forces of nature instead of feeling arrogant. They chant:

Lord of the lotus,
lord of the harvest,
Bright and munificent lord of the morn!
Thine is the bounty that prospered our sowing.[14]

These people are thanking the forces of nature for a bumper crop. They thank the God of Rain and the God of Corn for blessing them. They bring garlands and a portion of their crop to express their gratitude. In the same poem, Naidu also presents women's voices. Here, women like their male counterparts, are praying to mother Earth. They are thanking her for her kindness. They are thanking her for the wonderful crop that they have been blessed with. She writes:

Queen of the gourd-flower,
queen of the harvest,
Sweet and omnipotent mother, O Earth!
Thine is the plentiful bosom that feeds us,
Thine is the womb where our riches have birth.[15]

Likewise, in "Cradle Song," Naidu portrays a mother who is singing a lullaby and rocking her kid to sleep. Her song is full of descriptions of nature. She talks about groves, fields, birds and wind. What Naidu is probably trying to convey is that such a lullaby, if constantly repeated, will make little kids familiar with nature. This very child will grow up while remaining more conscious about the sanctity of the environment. Naidu writes:

[14] Naidu, *The Golden Threshold*, 16
[15] Naidu, *The Golden Threshold*, 16

From groves of spice,
O'er fields of rice,
Athwart the lotus-stream,
I bring for you,
Aglint with dew
A little lovely dream.[16]

How far Indian consciousness is rooted in nature is also revealed in
"Suttee." Here, a wife has lost her husband. She is lamenting. Her grief is
above any other sorrow of the world. In the Indian context, widowhood was
regarded as a curse. A widow was supposed to undergo multiple prescriptions
by society and religion. Her life became a living hell. Here, the speaker
decides not to live the life of a widow. She decides to perform suttee, which
means that she will leave this world and follow her husband into the other
world. The tone of the entire poem is sombre. Despite all this, the metaphors
of the speaker come from nature. It indicates that the Indian sensibility is
deeply rooted in nature in all circumstances. Here, the speaker, who happens
to be the wife of the deceased, likens him to a tree and herself to the blossom
of the tree. She speaks assertively:

Tree of my life,
Death's cruel foot
Hath crushed thee down to thy hidden root;
Nought shall restore thy glory fled.
Shall the blossom live when the tree is dead?[17]

Naidu's love poetry is conventional as far as the presentation of nature
is concerned. Like other love lyrics of other cultures and times, her speakers
also bring in nature to eulogise the beauty of their beloved. They also invoke
nature to compare their beloved's eyes, ears, nose, hair etc. for example, in
"Humayun to Zobeida," the lover equates his beloved's presence and appeal
to natural surroundings. He recalls various scenes from nature to express the
impact of her beauty on him. His admiration is intense and impassioned.
Here, nature also plays her part. It corroborates that an Indian expression is
incomplete without reference to nature irrespective of its context. The lover
sings enthusiastically:

You flaunt your beauty in the rose,
your glory in the dawn,

---

[16] Naidu, *The Golden Threshold*, 18
[17] Naidu, *The Golden Threshold*, 18

Your sweetness in the nightingale,
your whiteness in the swan.[18]

This note of exaggeration continues in "The Song of Princess Zeb-Un-Nissa." Here, the speaker is the princess herself. She is extremely beautiful. She is singing her own praise. Her tone is sometimes narcissistic and at other times boastful. She equates herself with all beautiful scenes of nature. She thinks that when she unveils herself, roses become envious. When she lets her tresses wave in the wind, the hyacinths complain and languish in vain. When she sings in the woods, nightingales grow weary. This is how she expresses herself:

When from my cheek I lift my veil,
The roses turn with envy pale,
And from their pierced hearts, rich with pain,
Send forth their fragrance like a wail.[19]

Like Keats, Naidu has also written a poem dedicated to autumn. In "Autumn Song," she differs significantly from her British counterpart. She does not eulogise autumn as the season of mellow fruitfulness. Her autumn is the season of decay and loss. She does not hail it as a season of various sights, scenes and sounds like Keats. Her approach is traditional. For her, autumn is the time of death and disintegration. She unfolds a scene where there is sadness all around and leaves are withering and flying away. The Sun is setting and hanging on the clouds. The lover is forlorn and jilted. There is neither any hope nor any desire left for him. He likens his situation with the leaves that are fallen and carried away by the wind. This is how Naidu weaves this tragic loss:

'My heart is weary and sad and alone,
For its dreams like the fluttering leaves have gone,
And why should I stay behind?'[20]

Likewise, in "Village Song," she presents a simple village girl on an errand who has lost her way back to home and is afraid as night is thickening around her. Here, Naidu unfolds the simple and straightforward lifestyle of Indian villagers that is permeated with interaction and dependence upon nature. As V. K. Gokak remarks that introduction of Indian themes has added more vitality to Naidu's verses. The protagonist, in the above-

---

[18] Naidu, *The Golden Threshold*, 20
[19] Naidu, *The Golden Threshold*, 22
[20] Naidu, *The Golden Threshold*, 20

mentioned poem, has gone out to fill her pots with water for daily requirements. When the poem opens, it is night and very late. The speaker is tense and jittery. She is cursing herself for stopping to listen to the song of a boat man whom one can presume to be her lover. As the night gets denser and darker, the speaker is beset with doubts and anxieties. She chants:

> Swiftly the shadows of night are falling,
> Hear, O hear, is the white crane calling,
> Is it the wild owl's cry?
> There are no tender moonbeams to light. (Gokak 1970, 150)[21]

She keeps thinking about her parents and siblings. In her prayers, there is nature. In her doubts, there is nature. In her hopes, there is nature. In her worries, there is nature. In her conjectures, there is nature. Whatever she thinks or sings, she cannot avoid giving reference to nature. She sings rather dolefully:

> The Jamuna's waters are deep'. . .
> The Jamuna's waters rush by so quickly,
> The shadows of evening gather so thickly,
> Like black birds in the sky. . . (Gokak 1970, 150)[22]

As John Felstiner questions, can poetry save the Earth? He later quotes John Keats who once remarked that, "The poetry of the earth is never dead. As long as there is Earth, poetry will survive."[23]

As the Earth has undergone various changes so has poetry. Everything from diction to form related to poetry has been metamorphosed to suit the modern-day requirements. Poems of Naidu are no aberration in this context. Even though they were written almost a hundred years back, they are still fresh and topical. One can easily identify with Naidu's verses as it reciprocates the call for action in modern times of eco-disasters. To quote Louise Westling and John Parham:

> In this millennial era, we appear to be in an ever-deepening environmental crisis. The era has been characterised as the Anthropocene in the formal geological sense of human action effecting stratigraphic change within rock

---

[21] Gokak, Vinayaka Krishna, editor, *The Golden Treasury of Indo-Anglian Poetry: 1828-1965*, (New Delhi: Sahitya Akademi, 1970), 150

[22] Gokak, *The Golden Treasury of Indo-Anglian Poetry: 1828-1965*, 150

[23] Felstiner, John. 2009. Can Poetry Save the Earth: A Field Guide to Nature Poetry. New Haven: Yale UP.

formations that will be visible to future geologists. More generally, it defines a period marked by interrelated, potentially cataclysmic human environmental impacts.[24]

As bush fires, mighty storms, deadly quakes, unpredictable weather patterns, extinction of birds and animals, deforestation, water, and air pollution are becoming more frequent, Naidu's poems present a more holistic and harmonious way of coexistence. Naidu paints mouth-watering images from the natural world. While reading her poems, one feels like passing through a forest, climbing over a mountain, bathing in the rain, basking in the sun, dancing in a garden, chasing the wind, listening to the chirping of the birds, and sitting on the clear banks of a river. Her poems are a bitter reminder for the contemporary capitalists and consumerists about what we had and what we have lost. To top it all, she champions Indian sensibility through her poems which can provide direction and solution to eco-disasters of today. Her poems are both backward looking and forward looking. In presenting the traditional Indian sensibility, she looks backwards in time when India was dominated by agriculture and animist beliefs. She is forward looking when she preserves Indian values through her poems for her posterity. These values promote the concept of harmony, symbiosis, and mutual dependence, as is revealed in the above analysis.

In short, Naidu's poems present nature in its vivid forms. With the passage of time, her appeal has widened and has acquired cosmopolitan significance. She portrays nature as both text and context. In her verses, nature is alive and active. Her protagonists are steeped in their natural environment. Moreover, Naidu is subtly conscious of her Indian heritage. She records her Indian values in relation to nature and other human beings quite astutely in her lyrics. Her poems are as relevant today as they were when they were composed decades ago. At that time, her poems inspired all Indians to be united, and channelled in them the spirit of nationalism against the colonial masters. These same Indian values and ethics can motivate everyone today to remain united in saving the Earth.

---

[24] Westling, Louise and John Parham, editors, *The Global History of Literature and the Environment.* (Cambridge: Cambridge UP, 2016), 1

Bibliography

Dwivedi, A. N. "Sarojini—the Poet (Born February 13,1879)." *Indian Literature*, (vol. 22, no. 3, 1979), pp. 115–126, www.jstor.org/stable/23329992.

Felstiner, John. 2009. *Can Poetry Save the Earth: A Field Guide to Nature Poetry*. New Haven: Yale UP.

Fisher, Michael. *An Environmental History of India: From Earliest Times to the Twenty-First Century*. (Cambridge: Cambridge UP, 2018).

Garrard, Greg, *Ecocriticism*, (Haryana: Replika Press Pvt. Ltd., 2007).

Glotfelty, Cheryll and Fromm, Harold, editors, *The Ecocriticism Reader: Landmarks in Literary Ecology*, (Georgia: U of Georgia P., 1996).

Gokak, Vinayaka Krishna, editor, *The Golden Treasury of Indo-Anglian Poetry: 1828- 1965*, (New Delhi: Sahitya Akademi, 1970).

Naidu, Sarojini and Symons, Arthur, *The Golden Threshold: With an Introduction by Arthur Symons,* (London: William Heinemann, 1905).

Sivaramakrishnan, Murali, "Ecopoetics and the Literature of Ancient India". In *A Global History of Literature and the Environment,* edited by John Parham and Louise Westling, (Cambridge: Cambridge UP, 2016), 65-79.

Westling, Louise and John Parham, editors, *The Global History of Literature and the Environment*. (Cambridge: Cambridge UP, 2016).

CHAPTER SEVEN

"SOMETHING COARSE AND CONCEALED": VIOLENT MYTHOLOGY AND ECOLOGICAL SUBVERSION IN WILLA CATHER'S *A LOST LADY*

ARUSH PANDE

Willa Cather's 1923 novel *A Lost Lady* is particularly resonant amidst late-stage capitalism—a stage characterised by the pervasive commodification of the environment, trapping its subjects in a language ill-equipped to imagine an ecological community of humans and nonhumans that is not undergirded by relations of human ownership and profit. "[G]rammar," Timothy Morton argues, "lines up against speaking about ecological beings."[1] He proceeds to implicate capitalist economic theory, which considers anything "outside of human social space…to be a mere 'externality'" and fails to account for the ways in which human and nonhuman beings "organise enjoyment with reference to one another."[2] The problem, in other words, is not that humans have drawn benefit, for pleasure or sustenance, from the nonhuman world. Mutually vitalising and pleasurable exchanges form the character of ecology. The problem is that our linguistic imagination, in the process of making these exchanges legible, consistently reproduces and reifies a set of relations in which humans emerge as owners and sole beneficiaries of the nonhuman world. To imagine an ecological community—one that focuses on how humans can thrive in *solidarity* with, as opposed to how they can most efficiently *utilise*, nonhuman beings—we need to struggle with the limits of language and find radical ways of

---

[1] Morton, Timothy, *Humankind: Solidarity with Non-Human People*, (London, Verso, 2017), 13

[2] Morton, Timothy, *Humankind: Solidarity with Non-Human People*, 14

narrating our relationship with the nonhuman world. In *A Lost Lady*, Cather offers one such narrative possibility.

Cather wrote against the backdrop of a mutating economic and social order—the passing of the age of the "pioneer" and the emergence of full-scale industrial capitalism, embodied by the establishment of transcontinental railroads. The figure of the pioneer, imagined as a noble visionary whose spirit is characterised by dreams of creation and adventure, is credited with the project of American nationalist expansion, involving the colonisation of the "wilderness"—land inhabited by Native American folks—beyond the national frontier. *A Lost Lady* grapples with the decline of the pioneer by tracing Niel Herbert's journey from adolescence to adulthood as he reckons with shifting economic contours around him. These shifts are marked primarily by the fading prosperity of a pioneer household whose lives and values he idolises. The pioneering figure is Captain Daniel Forrester, a railroad contractor who has worked for the Burlington Railroad company before settling down at Sweet Water, the town where Niel has grown up.[3] Niel is taken in by the Captain's mythical glory, and in particular, by his young wife Marian, who appears to him as impeccably charming. This charm, though, gradually fades with the Forrester's financial decline and Niel begrudges Marian for her failure to uphold the "aesthetic ideal" of a pioneer lady.[4] Indeed, closer to the novel's end, Cather writes that Niel most resented Marian because she "was not willing to immolate herself, like a widow of all these great men, and die with the pioneer period to which she belonged; that she preferred life on any terms."[5]

Such moments in the text have led some critics to interpret *A Lost Lady* as a novel that mourns Marian Forrester's "betrayal of the noble pioneer values of the [American] West."[6] Cather is presumed to have shared Niel's disillusionment with Marian. Charmion Gustke, for instance, draws on a letter that Cather exchanged with her mother to contend that she, like Niel, disapproves of Marian's changing disposition in the novel.[7] According to Gustke, Cather wrote this letter as an attempt to reconcile with her mother, who disapproved of Cather's "compassionate regard" for a certain Mrs. Garber, the woman whose "questionable choices" had reportedly inspired *A Lost Lady*.[8] Ironically, it is Gustke's choice of evidence that begs to be

[3] Cather, Willa, *A Lost Lady*, (London, Virago Press, 1923), 6
[4] Cather, *A Lost Lady*, 78
[5] Cather, *A Lost Lady*, 162
[6] Rosowski, Susan J. "Willa Cather's *A Lost Lady*: The Paradoxes of Change." *Novel: A Forum on Fiction,* (Vol. 11, No. 1, Duke University Press, 1977), 51
[7] Cather, *A Lost Lady*, 170
[8] Cather, *A Lost Lady*, 170

questioned. A letter written by Cather to resolve a conflict and placate her mother is hardly the most reliable or conclusive measure of what the author *truly* felt.[9] Besides, it is fallacious to claim that all of Cather's opinions should map onto her writing coherently. In "Willa Cather's *A Lost Lady*: The Paradoxes of Change," Susan J. Rosowski cautions against such interpretations of the novel which bear the risk of "fitting the individual work into the pre-conceived framework."[10] Rosowki acknowledges that "the reader must distinguish Niel's criteria for [Marian Forrester] from those that emerge from Cather's characterisation of her."[11] Yet, her call for an interpretive distance from Niel's perspective fails to question the common assumption among critics that Cather's novel portrays "the pioneering spirit" as "noble."[12] Putting pressure on this assumption, I argue that while *A Lost Lady* participates in the iconography of the pioneer myth, it simultaneously critiques this myth through its unreliable narrative, which Cather inflects with notes of cognitive dissonance. These dissonant notes, often painfully ironic, bear witness to Marian's suffering—a violent effect of the role ordained for her in the social relations governed and ideologically obscured by the pioneer myth. Marian, however, is not the only survivor of the myth's violence. Cather's use of analogies between Marian and the nonhuman elements of the Captain's estate—for instance, the groves, the marsh, and the livestock—exposes the pioneer's role in ecological injuries to the nonhuman world.

My reading of *A Lost Lady* is a departure from the work of critics who have, over the last twenty years, become interested in Cather's environmentalism. An ecocritical approach to Cather has a lot to promise, but so far this work has traced Cather's environmental thought to the pioneer's aesthetic and spiritual regard for the "natural" world.[13] I contend, instead, that Cather's critique of the figure of the pioneer in *A Lost Lady* lends itself to a far more sophisticated ecological politics. In presenting Marian and the Captain's estate as respective measures for the misogynistic and ecological injuries experienced by the other, *A Lost Lady* enacts a subversive ecological relation at the formal level. In this relation, the

---

[9] Cather, *A Lost Lady*, 170

[10] Rosowski, "Willa Cather's *A Lost Lady*: The Paradoxes of Change," 51

[11] Cather, *A Lost Lady*, 55

[12] Rosowski, "Willa Cather's *A Lost Lady*: The Paradoxes of Change," 62

[13] Nadir, Leila C. "Time Out of Place: Modernity and the Rise of Environmentalism in Willa Cather's *O Pioneers!*" *Cather Studies, Volume 10*: Willa Cather and the Nineteenth Century, edited by Anne L. Kaufman and Richard H. Millington, (University of Nebraska Press, 2015), 78

Captain's human wife and nonhuman estate form an ecological community characterised by mutual good.

I. The Lady and the Landscape

Why does Marian Forrester become the locus of Niel's anxieties about fading pioneer glory? This question calls for a closer look at Marian's relation to Captain Forrester's image as the pioneer. Cather explores this relation in an early episode in the novel when the Captain recounts his dream about a house at Sweet Water: "I planned to build a house that my friends could come to, with a wife like Mrs. Forrester to make it attractive to them."[14] Following a series of chapters that foreground her charming effect on the Forrester place, this line appears like a reference to Marian Forrester. The subsequent paragraph, though, qualifies that the Captain is "referring to his first marriage," instead of his second one with Marian.[15] The revelation elicits confusion and surprise. To begin with, the Captain's mode of address is ambiguous and could indicate two different people, a possibility that the subsequent qualification attests to. That the expression "Mrs. Forrester" has, so far in the novel, referred exclusively to Marian and never the Captain's unnamed first wife, makes this moment more conspicuous. The novel, by abruptly introducing the first wife as a referent for "Mrs. Forrester," orchestrates confusion around the address, drawing attention to the substitutability of the two wives—the two Mrs. Forresters— in the Captain's dream. Marian is undoubtedly central in realising this dream and thereby cementing the mythical verve of his pioneering spirit. She can play charming in front of his friends far better than the previous Mrs. Forrester, whom they remember as "the poor invalid wife who had never been happy and who had kept his nose to the grindstone."[16] Yet, paradoxically, Marian finds no mention in the Captain's recollection; she is completely overshadowed by the figure she performs and represents. It is this figure of the "charming wife" that assumes significance for Captain Forrester. Her 'real' identity need not be spelled out, accounting for no more than a narrative afterthought.

The wife features in the Captain's "plan" as additional construction—an accessory, like a porch or a balcony—that the house must be built "*with...* to make it attractive to*" his friends (emphasis mine). In this respect, Mrs. Forrester resembles the nonhuman elements of the environment that

---

[14] Cather, *A Lost Lady*, 48
[15] Cather, *A Lost Lady*, 48
[16] Cather, *A Lost Lady*, 48

enhance the otherwise "not at all remarkable" Forrester place with a "certain charm of atmosphere."[17] Captain Forrester regards her, like the well, the grove, and the orchard, as an aesthetic feature of his house. The novel compares the pleasure that the Captain experiences from witnessing Mrs. Forrester's mesmerising effect on his male friends to his gratification on hearing them "admire his fine stock, grazing in the meadows."[18] The resemblance persists in Niel's first-hand experience of the Forrester place. Niel's expressions of delight as he, barely conscious, soaks in the atmosphere of Mrs. Forrester's bedroom, oscillate between describing the Captain's wife and the physical environment of his house:

> What soft fingers Mrs. Forrester had, and what a lovely lady she was. Inside the lace ruffle of her dress he saw her white throat rising and falling so quickly […]. *The little boy was thinking he would probably never be in so nice a place again.* The windows went almost down to the baseboard… and the closed green shutters let in streaks of sunlight that quivered on the polished floor and the silver things on the dresser […]. The massive walnut furniture was all inlaid with pale-coloured woods […]. Mrs. Forrester ran her fingers through his black hair and lightly kissed him on the forehead. Oh, how sweet, how sweet she smelled! (emphasis mine)[19]

The narrator's use of a spatial expression—"so nice a place"—to describe the young boy's state is striking. Niel receives Marian's charm, the magnificent shimmer of the sunlight, and the finely inlaid furniture similarly—as features of the Forrester house working harmoniously to overwhelm and enchant him. The force of these analogies, peppered across the text, rests in their sophistication. Cather does not compare Marian to the nonhuman environment of the Captain's estate in any essential way that might run the risk of reproducing simplistic myths about "the nature of women" or "nature as a woman." What she analogises is the semiotic positions—the symbolic meanings—of Marian and the nonhuman estate within the iconography of Captain Forrester, which repurpose them as aesthetic mannequins servicing his pioneer aura.

Analogy is a particularly useful literary device here because it represents the tension between similarity and difference. By claiming that two or more markedly distinct things are actually comparable in a specific context, analogies can expose the arbitrariness of semiotic positions through cognitive dissonance. Cather's analogous representation of Marian and the nonhuman

---

[17] Cather, *A Lost Lady*, 5, 6
[18] Cather, *A Lost Lady*, 7, 8
[19] Cather, *A Lost Lady*, 24

elements of the estate sometimes produce such dissonant effects. For instance, despite the resonance that Cather crafts, there is something disruptive and unsettling about Marian Forrester, a lively and vibrant young woman, being compared with immobile pieces of furniture. In a way, I attempt to mirror that effect when I describe her, a few lines before, as a mannequin. In both cases, the unsettling effect results because Marian is represented in a form that contradicts the way she is described throughout the novel. It is painful to imagine that someone known for their vitality and dynamism serves the same purpose to a mythical project as objects conventionally viewed as static or lifeless. Cather's occasionally dissonant analogies illuminate how the Captain's pioneer aura constricts Marian in a representational trap. The mythology of the pioneer, quite literally, objectifies her.

II. The Myth and Its Injuries

Among critics who have responded to *A Lost Lady*, Nina Schwartz constitutes a notable exception because of her skeptical attitude towards the pioneer myth. Unlike respondents who agree with the narrative of "America's decline from her grand past," Schwartz reads, in the novel, a kind of ancestral continuity between the mythologized pioneer era and the petty and materialistic culture of capitalistic exchange that follows.[20] She, too, marks dissonances in the narrative, albeit different ones from those that I have reflected on, to argue that "despite its complicity in such mythologization, *A Lost Lady* exposes both the mechanisms by which it distorts certain historical actualities and the interests in whose service it operates."[21] Schwartz's intervention is productive but incomplete. Cather's novel not only exposes the mythologization of history involved in constructing the figure of the pioneer, but also provides an affective measure for the violence it unleashes on bodies like Marian and the nonhuman world. This affective measure becomes accessible through the novel's detailing of Niel's interactions with and emotional responses to Captain Forrester and Marian.

Niel is seduced by the pioneer myth—by the dream that the Captain has envisioned and realised—and yet, aware of his own improbable odds of emulating it. He experiences the Captain's house and all its pleasures simultaneously as "so nice a place" and one that "he would probably never

---

[20] Schwartz, Nina. "History and the Invention of Innocence in *A Lost Lady.*" *Arizona Quarterly: A Journal of American Literature, Culture, and Theory*, (Vol. 46, No. 2, University of Arizona Press, 1990), 34

[21] Schwartz, "History and the Invention of Innocence in *A Lost Lady*," 34

be in" again. His thoughts about the elusiveness of this place, the physical manifestation of the Captain's mythical pioneer life, follow a recollection of his own house, "where everything was horrid when one was sick."[22] Niel, by ascribing a scarce, fleeting quality to this fantasy, both intensifies his attachment to it and displaces the source of his pleasure onto Captain Forrester's experience of it. Lacking any entitlement to the Forrester place, he reaffirms the fantasy by directing his attachment to the Captain's revelry in his entitlement.[23] The novel registers this effect by narrating Niel's observation of the Captain surveying his estate: "He stood looking out through the glass at the drifted shrubbery. Niel *liked* to see him look out over his place. A man's house is *his castle*, the look seemed to say" (emphases mine).[24] For Niel, the Captain's look indicates that his property is like a "castle," representing a form of ownership that bears both the mythical aura of royal legacy and the fortified air of exclusivity. This form of ownership becomes a source of vicarious satisfaction for Niel, which is replicated in his admiration of Marian, who is most fascinating to him "as Captain Forrester's wife and in relation to her husband."[25] Her "other charming attributes," hold value for him only to the extent that they make her supposed "loyalty to him" appear exceptional.[26] Niel indexes Marian's worth through her affirmation of the Captain's right to exclusively possess her.

Ironically, Niel's own loyalty to the Captain is undercut by his position as Marian's confidante in the novel. The first visible instance of her infidelity occurs on Niel's watch, albeit unbeknownst to him. Before disappearing into the woods with her lover Frank Ellinger, she entrusts Niel to take care of the possible obstruction in Constance Ogden, parting with "a meaning, *confidential* smile" (emphasis mine).[27] The muted gesture of trust and secrecy foreshadows later moments in the novel, when Niel finds himself reluctantly offering a space for Marian to voice safely thoughts she cannot air publicly. Her intoxicated meltdown involving a confession about her affair with Ellinger takes place in Niel's presence.[28] More significantly though, it is to Niel that Marian expresses repeated dissatisfaction with her life at Sweet Water. She tells him that "she can't stand this house a moment

---

[22] Cather, *A Lost Lady*, 24
[23] For a greater exposition of loss and displacement, *see*: Freud, "Mourning and Melancholia."
[24] Cather, *A Lost Lady*, 66-67
[25] Cather, *A Lost Lady*, 71
[26] Cather, *A Lost Lady*, 71-72
[27] Cather, *A Lost Lady*, 55
[28] Cather, *A Lost Lady*, 127

longer" Once animated by her vitality, the place strikes her with anxieties of stagnation: "'Oh, but it is bleak!" she *murmured.* 'Suppose we have to stay here all next winter, too... and the next! What will become of me, Niel?'" There was fear, unmistakeable fright in her voice" (emphasis mine).[29] Her chilling perspective dispels the glory around the Forrester estate and, instead, offers a grim picture of the restraint and confinement she experiences and fears. Even her revelation takes the form of a murmur, as if something stifles her speech. Her suggestion that the Captain might himself be a controlling and authoritative figure is similarly held back—indicated briefly when she waits for him to fall asleep before proposing a harmless run down the hill, because there would be "no one to stop us. No objections!"[30] As both devotee to the Captain's pioneer image and witness to Marian's moving counter narrative, Niel finds himself in a precarious position that demands the negotiation of recurring emotional conflict.

Cather represents this negotiation by juxtaposing scenes where Marian confides in Niel with his glaring oversights in reading them. Niel registers Marian's words in his memory but misappropriates them to uphold the ideal he is devoted to—"of a man like the railroad builder, her loyalty to him"— which, he believes, "could never become worn or shabby."[31] The novel details the process of this mythologization:

> He rather *liked* the stories, even the spiteful ones, about the gay life she led in Colorado, and the young men she kept dangling about her every winter. He sometimes thought of the life she might have been living ever since he had known her and the one she had *chosen* to live. From that disparity, *he believed*, came the subtlest thrill of her fascination. (emphases mine)[32]

This moment is impregnated by a skillful demonstration of narrative irony because Niel's reading of the situation is wrong on every count. To begin with, the novel has already established Marian's infidelity; the loyalty that Niel thinks "could never become worn or shabby" was sullied while he innocently kept company with Constance Ogden. Additionally, the conversation that precedes this moment makes it evident that Marian had not "chosen" the life at Sweet Water over her "gay life" in Colorado. If anything, she actively mourns her inability to escape Sweet Water for Colorado and the thought of not being able to leave, winter after winter, fills

---

[29] Cather, *A Lost Lady,* 70
[30] Cather, *A Lost Lady,* 70
[31] Cather, *A Lost Lady,* 71-72
[32] Cather, *A Lost Lady,* 72

her with "unmistakable fright."[33] Yet, Niel *finds* a way to mistake this fear for a noble choice. Cather chooses this moment to make a rare narrative qualification. She explicitly distances the novel's perspective from Niel. "[H]e believed," not necessarily the novel, that disparity between the life Marian could have led and the one she found herself trapped in held some kind of superlative thrill.

The sharp cognitive dissonance achieved by this scene gradually begins to register the effects of the pioneer myth on Marian at an affective level. What does it mean for Marian's closest confidante in the novel—a person she entrusts with her private feelings—to not only blatantly ignore her fears, but to enjoy hearing about them, seeking in them a thrilling affirmation of his own attachments? "In the eyes of the admiring middle-aged men" devoted to Captain Forrester, "whatever Mrs. Forrester chose to do was lady-like because she did it."[34] This line summarises the cruelty of the myth of the pioneer, the "something coarse and concealed" that feeds its beauty. The pioneer myth erases Marian to preserve Lady Forrester, robbing her experiences and desires of the power to signify beyond its ideological matrix.

It is true, indeed, that these mournful expressions of desire for escape and a better life are also mediated through privileges lent to Marian by the same economic system that constrains her. Schwartz is troubled by the novel's sympathetic regard for these feelings of loss: "[T]he narrative itself expresses some bitterness about the lost world that Marian seems to represent. [I]t does seem to mourn the loss of that earlier life of gracious ease that she had lived; and such nostalgia is, I think, as dangerous and deluded as Niel's judgment of his lost lady."[35] While Schwartz's warning about the potential for this kind of nostalgia to distract from the critique of the pioneer myth demands serious consideration, it is equally imperative to acknowledge that this nostalgia is what lends the critique its affective force. It is through this nostalgic mourning for what Marian has lost that the novel is able to articulate the injuries she has borne. The sentimental regard for that loss, the "unmistakable fright" of stagnation it causes her, is necessary to make apparent the cruel irony of Niel's repeated misreading in service of his attachment to the Captain's mythical glory. While Marian is always being appropriated in service of the myth—starting from the moment she becomes a part of the Captain's plan to build a house at Sweet Water, it is in the novel's misguided nostalgia for Marian's lost life of "gracious ease" that the injuries to her begin to reverberate emotionally. The myth of the

---

[33] Cather, *A Lost Lady*, 70
[34] Cather, *A Lost Lady*, 8
[35] Cather, *A Lost Lady*, 45

pioneer chokes Marian with the very necklace it rewards her with. Her status as a beneficiary of the old economic order is not incommensurate with the violence it unleashes on her life and legibility.

This violence surfaces quite explicitly when Niel realises that Marian prefers "life on any terms" and is not, like him, hopelessly devoted to the pioneer. Unable to sustain his fantasy about Marian and desperate to preserve his attachment to the myth, Niel is flooded by an impulse to watch Marian "immolate herself like a widow" of all pioneers.[36] The implication, admittedly, is metaphorical. Niel does not want her to burn; he wishes her to stagnate with the values of the pioneer era rather than mould herself to the ensuing changes in the socioeconomic system. Yet, Cather's reference to Niel's hunger for this act of self-immolation describes the manic violence that underlies his impulse to symbolically control Marian. In his enchantment under the myth, Niel has come to bear an uncanny resemblance to the man he detests all his life—the unscrupulous Ivy Peters who kills dogs and tortures birds for his amusement. The destructive rage and fervour he feels towards Marian becomes a telling indicator of the magnitude of violence that the myth can generate.

III. A New Language for Ecological Injury

The semiotic violence of the pioneer myth is not solely directed at Marian. It also, as discussed earlier, traps the nonhuman environment which constitutes the Captain's property in a similar matrix of meaning. The similarity of these two cases of semiotic circumscription is what, in the first place, exposes the objectification of Marian. This awareness itself can permit reasonable speculation about ecological injury, but it cannot account for the absence of a reliable measure to perceive the violence experienced by the nonhuman environment. Cather offers an incisive view into the ways in which violence to the nonhuman becomes perceptible when, early in the novel, she describes the scene where Niel and his young friends watch Ivy Peters mutilate a woodpecker:

"He held the woodpecker's head in a vise made of his thumb and forefinger. [A]s if it were a practiced trick, with one of those tiny blades he slit both the eyes that glared in the bird's stupid little head, and instantly released it [...]. The boys stood watching it, indignant and uncomfortable, not knowing what to do. *They were not especially sensitive; Thad was always on hand when there was anything doing at the slaughterhouse, and the Blum boys lived by killing things. They wouldn't have believed they could be so upset by a hurt*

---

[36] Cather, *A Lost Lady*, 162

woodpecker. There was something wild and desperate about the way the darkened creature beat its wings in the branches, whirling in the sunlight and never seeing it...." (emphasis mine)[37]

This moment unearths the limits and possibilities of language in making nonhuman injury perceptible. The violence only becomes evident through an appeal to human emotions. It is not the mere fact of the woodpecker's injury, but the resemblance of its effect with the emotional state of desperation, that upsets the boys. On a more hopeful note, though, this emotional resonance holds the potential to defamiliarize forms of violence that one has normalised. It is no coincidence that reflecting on the boys' discomfort simultaneously allows Cather to suggest that their quotidian acts of "killing things" also ensconced violence, even if they "were not especially sensitive" to it.

This brings the full extent of Cather's intervention to light. In this novel, she actually goes beyond intuiting that the modern economic order and its consubstantial pioneer mythology might be injurious to Marian and the nonhuman environment of the Captain's estate. Through her attentive exploration of the emotional effects that this mythologised system of ownership produces on Marian, Cather offers an affective index to perceive and assess the ways in which it violates the nonhuman. For instance, the full extent of ecological injury to the marsh on the Forrester property becomes evident through its resonance with Marian. Both Marian and the marsh are caught between competing ownership claims—Niel's impulsive guardianship and Ivy's "petty economics" of exchange.[38] Neither Ivy, who exploits Marian to spite the Captain (and his memory), nor Niel, who is committed to preserving her as an unsullied "aesthetic ideal," is able to value her outside "her relation to her husband." This conflict is echoed in Cather's description of the draining of the marsh: Niel "felt that Ivy had drained the marsh as much to spite him... as to reclaim the land [...]. By draining the marsh, Ivy had obliterated a few acres of something he had hated, though he could not name it, and had exerted his power over the people who had loved these unproductive meadows for their idleness and silvery beauty."[39] The marsh, like Marian, becomes collateral—a mere playing field—to the tussle between Niel's aggressive love and Ivy's aggressive hate for the Captain's entitlement and everything it represents. Both of them fail to value the marsh outside modes of ownership and their accompanying myths. This erasure is so powerful that even critics like

---

[37] Cather, *A Lost Lady*, 21
[38] Cather, *A Lost Lady*, 77, 100
[39] Cather, *A Lost Lady*, 99-100

Schwartz, who have observed the resonance, have failed to spot it. "Indeed, both the marsh and Marian," Schwartz writes, "are examples of artifice, not nature: though the marsh may look as if it were a remnant of untouched prairie, its existence is an effect of the Captain's money and of the aesthetic pleasure he takes in" it.[40] Schwartz is correct in her assessment of the marsh as artifice to the extent that, as the Captain's property, it is reduced to an aesthetic artefact representing an illusory past. This, however, is not the only valuable form in which the marsh exists. Even in times when the Captain's economic ownership over it is uncontested, it forms a vital ecosystem that sustains weeds and mud snakes. The characters' inability to represent this form of value is, conspicuously, a far cry from the way Cather understood ecological networks. In Willa Cather's *Ecology of Place*, Rosowski observes, "Far from dismissing nature as a conventional backdrop, Cather was reading drama in the vegetation about her: winds blow *over bluffs*, and as if in stealthy attack, yellow scorch *creeps* down tender inside leaves about the ear of corn" (emphases hers).[41] Evidently, Cather was deeply conscious of the animated character of even non-sentient bodies and life forms. By juxtaposing mythic representations of the marsh as an unproductive landscape reflective of idle beauty against brief, scattered mentions of the marsh—a space animated by snakes, weeds, and birds—as a vital site for nonhuman *re*production in the novel, Cather elevates the marsh to the status of a tragic character. It becomes a survivor, like Marian, of the pioneer's violence on the prairie.

A Lost Lady articulates the misogynistic and ecological injuries of the pioneer myth by using Marian and elements of the Captain's nonhuman estate as measures for accounting one another's trauma. This mutually valuable relationship represents a subversive alternative to the two corrosive stages of capitalist ownership at play in the novel: the "pioneer" stage and the stage of "petty" commodity exchange. The novel imagines Marian and the nonhuman estate as a robust ecological community without the concentration of benefit that characterises the prevailing systems it depicts. Most significantly, this subversive ecological relation is created entirely by Cather. In other words, there is nothing in the narrative world of the novel to indicate that Marian or the nonhuman estate might share affinities with and for one another in any conscious way.[42] The subversive ecological

---

[40] Schwartz, "History and the Invention of Innocence in *A Lost Lady*," 43
[41] Rosowski, "Willa Cather's *A Lost Lady*: The Paradoxes of Change," 51
[42] I sense the possibility for a case to be made about Marian's desire to escape into the 'wildernesses' beyond the Captain's estate when its oppressive affect seems to overbear her. The woods by the river where Marian and Frank have sex represent, for her, a space of sexual possibility outside her marriage. For more on the idea of

community formed by them is Cather's invention. It is in her telling of *A Lost Lady* as a story of individual and collective, patriarchal and ecological, traumas that this community comes to life and to light.

IV. I See Your Myth, I Raise You My Doubt: A Conclusion

In some ways, my argument is undermined by Cather's biography and public writings, both of which suggest an ostensibly unequivocal appreciation of the pioneer era and the social, economic, and historical order it comprised.[43] In her 1923 *Nation* essay, "Nebraska: The End of the First Cycle," she mourned that the "splendid story of the pioneers," who "subdued the wild land and broke up the virgin prairie" was "finished." This is the prevalent version of Cather in literary history, recurring in biographical as well as critical discussions of her work.

In "Ecology of Place," Rosowski tries to introduce "a Willa Cather we've scarcely met, the Cather who while growing up in Red Cloud went on rounds with Dr. McKeeby, observing him as he diagnosed and treated his patients; and the Cather who in her high school graduation speech described success as becoming a 'great anatomist or a brilliant naturalist.'"[44] She traces a foundational "ecological dialectic" across Cather's art and establishes her as an avid and well-informed student of botanical and environmental processes.[45] Building on this framework, Cheryl and John Swift, botanist and literary critic respectively, claim that Cather was more than just "a literary flower-lover." She was a "theorist of nature, engaged throughout her career with the conceptual complexities that formed modern plant science."[46]

It is fallacious and speculative to suggest that Cather's ecological awareness is incommensurate with and negates her captivation by the mythology of the pioneer. Equally, though, it is naïve to imagine that her writing would not capture any conflict between her deep regard for the so-called pioneers and her keen interest in the transforming effects of history

'wilderness' as 'queer' or subversive space, read Catriona Mortimer Sandilands and Bruce Erickson's introduction to *Queer Ecologies: Sex, Nature, Politics, Desire*.

[43] Nadir, "Time Out of Place: Modernity and the Rise of Environmentalism in Willa Cather's *O Pioneers!*", 68

[44] Rosowski, "Willa Cather's *A Lost Lady*: The Paradoxes of Change," 37

[45] Rosowski, "Willa Cather's *A Lost Lady*: The Paradoxes of Change," 42

[46] Swift, Cheryl C. and Swift, John N. "Willa Cather and American Plant Ecology." *Interdisciplinary Studies in Literature and Environment*, (Vol. 8, No. 2, Association for the Study of Literature and Environment, 2001), 1

on the environment.[47] The question that interests me is: Did Cather's ecological bent ever generate doubt about the myth of the pioneer? Interestingly, *A Lost Lady* emerged out of creative doubt. In a 1925 interview with Flora Merrill (now Flora Macdonald Denison), Cather reveals that she had initially written the novel from Niel's perspective: "I discarded ever so many drafts, and in the beginning wrote it in the first person, speaking as the boy himself. The question was, by what medium could I present her the most vividly, and that, of course, meant *the most truly* [...]. I had to succeed in this. Otherwise, I would have been *cheating...*" (emphases mine).[48] Niel's voice in the novel bears Cather's publicly expressed beliefs about the passing economic and social order. Yet, she chooses to mediate that perspective, feeling that it might not be the most accurate version of events, and that she might be "cheating" (someone or something?) by only narrating that version. The novel suggests that perhaps Cather was haunted by a "chilling doubt" similar to Niel's suspicion of beautiful women: that "the brilliancy of" the pioneer was "always fed by something coarse and concealed."[49] Her decision to write the novel in third-person, free-indirect discourse offers a corrective to Niel, expressing a willingness to dwell in her doubt instead of finding ways to bury it.

I do not present the subversive ecological politics of *A Lost Lady* as the product of entirely conscious thoughts. According to primacy to conscious thought, an anthropocentric construct, lends itself to a seriously limited ecological politics. Morton writes, "I cannot speak the ecological subject because language, and in particular grammar, is fossilized human thoughts."[50] He advocates "dropping the idea that (human) thought is the top access mode and holding that brushing against, licking or irradiating are also access modes as valid (or as invalid) as thinking."[51] Perhaps Cather only brushes against (or licks!) a subversive ecological relation, but she is able to play with her doubt and use her storytelling prowess to transgress semiotic borders. For better readers than Niel Herbert, there is hope in that.

---

[47] Nadir, "Time Out of Place: Modernity and the Rise of Environmentalism in Willa Cather's *O Pioneers!*", 73
[48] Cather, in Merrill
[49] Cather, *A Lost Lady*, 93, 79
[50] Morton, Timothy, *Humankind: Solidarity with Non-Human People*, (London, Verso, 2017), 13
[51] Morton, *Humankind: Solidarity with Non-Human People*, 18

Bibliography

Cather, Willa, *A Lost Lady*, (London, Virago Press, 1923).

—. "Nebraska: The End of the First Cycle," *The Willa Cather Archive*, https://cather.unl.edu/writings/nonfiction/nf066.

—. "'A Short Story Course Can Only Delay, It Cannot Kill an Artist,' Says Willa Cather," *The Willa Cather Archive*, https://cather.unl.edu/writings/bohlke/interviews/bohlke.i.21.

Gustke, Charmion. "The Trafficking of Mrs. Forrester: Prostitution and Willa Cather's *A Lost Lady*." *Cather Studies, Volume 11: Willa Cather at the Modernist Crux*, edited by Ann Mosley, John J. Murphy, and Robert Thacker, University of Nebraska Press, 2017, pp. 170-187.

Morton, Timothy, *Humankind: Solidarity with Non-Human People*, (London, Verso, 2017).

Nadir, Leila C. "Time Out of Place: Modernity and the Rise of Environmentalism in Willa Cather's *O Pioneers!*" *Cather Studies, Volume 10*: Willa Cather and the Nineteenth Century, edited by Anne L. Kaufman and Richard H. Millington, (University of Nebraska Press, 2015), pp. 68-96.

Rosowski, Susan J. "Willa Cather's *A Lost Lady*: The Paradoxes of Change." *Novel: A Forum on Fiction,* (Vol. 11, No. 1, Duke University Press, 1977), pp. 51-62.

—. "Willa Cather's Ecology of Place." *Western American Literature*, (Vol. 30, No. 1, University of Nebraska Press, 1995), pp. 37-51.

Schwartz, Nina. "History and the Invention of Innocence in *A Lost Lady*." *Arizona Quarterly: A Journal of American Literature, Culture, and Theory*, (Vol. 46, No. 2, University of Arizona Press, 1990), pp. 33-54.

Swift, Cheryl C. and Swift, John N. "Willa Cather and American Plant Ecology." *Interdisciplinary Studies in Literature and Environment*, (Vol. 8, No. 2, Association for the Study of Literature and Environment, 2001), pp. 1- 12.

CHAPTER EIGHT

KILLING THE SNAKE:
ATTACKING THE PATRIARCHY
IN CATHER'S *MY ÁNTONIA*

LAURA HOLDER

Some scholars consider Willa Cather's *My Ántonia* to be a transitional work because, beginning with this novel, she stops creating strong female characters. Deborah Lambert expresses this opinion in her article "The Defeat of a Hero: Autonomy and Sexuality in *My Ántonia*." Lambert claims that Cather abandons women in her later novels and focuses exclusively on "patriarchal institutions and predominantly male characters."[1] *My Ántonia* demonstrates this new focus by having Ántonia not be the central focus; instead, she is portrayed through Jim, a male narrator. Another factor is that she is all but absent from the latter half of the novel as an active character. Also, any strength of character that Ántonia has is relegated, by the end of the novel, to simply being a mother capable of producing strong sons. She holds no value as an individual but is instead set aside to become a nostalgic ideal of placid women in society.

For critics like Lambert, or even Blanche Gelfant, who expands the concept of Cather's abandonment not just of strong female characters but of sexual relations altogether, Cather's suspected homosexuality often comes into play. The documented cases of Cather's cross-dressing, refusal to marry, and long relationships with women, however platonic, have made critics believe she rejected writing about strong women because she herself identified more with the male role models in her field. There is another possible explanation for this seeming abandonment, however, using a

---

[1] Deborah G. Lambert, "The Defeat of a Hero: Autonomy and Sexuality in *My Ántonia*," *American Literature,* 53.4 (January 1982), 680.

concept called "narrative blank space."[2] As described by Terrence Martin in his article, "The Drama of Memory in *My Ántonia*," narrative blank space are voids in the story, spaces that are empty of authorial intent. These spaces, then, "afford little but material for conjecture and inference."[3] In other words, the lack of specific information in a narrative does not necessarily represent support for only what's there. As a blank space, it opens up more opportunities for the readers to create their own understandings. Martin uses this term to discuss the twenty-year break between Books IV and V of the novel. Patrick Shaw argues that this blank space is meant to raise questions rather than serve as a blunt statement. Likewise, the absence of strong female characters and, in the case of Gelfant's argument, sexual relations, in *My Ántonia* serves as a narrative blank space that should be questioned and examined rather than merely condemned as an abandonment of women by a repressed lesbian author.

What comes out of this narrative blank space is not an eschewal of women and the feminine sphere, but rather an attack on the ruling patriarchal society of the time. Michel Foucault, in *The History of Sexuality*, describes this idea as the "negative relation" in the principals of power.[4] The negative relation states that power provides boundaries and produces "absences and gaps," taking the "general form of limit and lack".[5] The negative relation within Cather's novels is reminiscent of the limiting power Cather struggled against as a female writer in a patriarchal field. This direct attack comes in the form of hyper-sexual metaphor and elements of castration as seen throughout the novel. The two most impressive scenes where Cather works not only to emasculate her male narrator, but society at large are the snake killing scene and the near rape scene with Wick Cutter. In both cases, the narrator, Jim, is castrated in a social sense, taking away his threat as a sexual male and making his relationship with Ántonia even stronger because he is no longer the sexually dominant male.

Cather sets up the basis for her attack on the patriarchy as soon as Jim arrives at his grandparents' home. The first day after his arrival, Jim is called to help his grandmother harvest potatoes in the family garden a quarter of a mile away from the house. On their way to the garden, the grandmother shows Jim her "rattlesnake cane," a "stout hickory cane, tipped with copper,

---

[2] Patrick W. Shaw, "*My Ántonia:* Emergence and Authorial Revelations," *American Literature* 56.4 (December 1984), 527.

[3] Terence Martin, "The Drama of Memory in *My Ántonia*," *PMLA*, 84.2 (March 1969), 308.

[4] Michel Foucault, *The History of Sexuality: An Introduction. Vol. I.* Trans. by Robert Hurley (New York: Vintage Books, 1990), 83.

[5] Foucault, 83.

which hung by a leather thong from her belt."[6] The cane, hanging from her belt at her hips functions not only as a phallic representation, also as a form of attack and castration. The grandmother warns Jim never to venture to the garden without a heavy stick or a corn-knife with which to beat or cut the heads off snakes, respectively. The grandmother finishes her warning by relating the story of a young girl who, having been "bitten on the ankle," has been "sick all summer."[7]

The fact that it is a female character expressing this warning against snakes and a female victim of a rattler's bite is very important for Cather's story. The snake, what Jim later refers to as the "Eldest of evil," serves as Cather's representative of masculinity and patriarchal power in society.[8] The little girl that has been ill during the summer from a snakebite represents the practice of the indoctrination of women into their place in society from a young age. Feminist critics Sandra Gilbert and Susan Gubar claim that many diseases or symptoms of disease can be traced back to the processes of "patriarchal socialization."[9] This education in "docility, submissiveness, [and] selflessness," claim Gilbert and Gubar, cannot help but cause sickness in women because it requires them to renounce their primal urge to their "*own* survival, pleasure [and] assertion."[10] The little girl, having been bitten by a snake, is forced to stay still and docile during the long summer months for her recovery. If she does not obey this period of forced submissiveness, then it is very likely she will die. However, if she survives her illness, then she will be ready to take her place in the domestic sphere because she will have had months of preparation at being quiet and subdued, giving up her own time and pleasure to fulfill the wishes of others.

When Jim and his grandmother finish their work, Jim asks to stay behind. His grandmother asks, "Aren't you afraid of snakes?"[11] Jim admits to being a little afraid but opts to stay anyway. Jim's fear of snakes, a phallic representation that Jim should identify and be enthralled with as a boy, sets him up as an already slightly emasculated individual. He is neither a stereotypical boy, nor is he a completely feminized male. Accepting his

---

[6] Willa Cather, *My Ántonia* (New York: Oxford University Press, 2006), 15.
[7] Cather, 15.
[8] Cather, 32.
[9] Sandra M. Gilbert and Susan Gubar. *The Madwoman in the Attic: The Woman Writer and the Nineteenth-Century Literary Imagination.* In *The Norton Anthology of Theory and Criticism*, ed. Vincent B. Leitch (New York: W.W. Norton & Company, 2001), 2030.
[10] Gilbert and Gubar, 2030.
[11] Cather, 16.

answer, his grandmother leaves him alone and Jim sits down in the middle of the garden, "where snakes could scarcely approach unseen."[12]

The garden acts as a sphere of feminine domesticity – it is a place of growth and birth. Though it is a place where snakes come and go, it is still a quiet, domestic space. Cather pulls from traditional Greek mythology, which places the earth and natural forces within the feminine realm. The garden and the act of the harvest, especially, are reminiscent of the goddess Demeter. Simone de Beauvoir argues that men have always seen women as being "related to nature."[13] "She incarnates it," says de Beauvoir, the "vale of blood, open rose, siren, the curve of a hill, she represents to man the fertile soil, the sap, the material beauty and soul of the world."[14] This connection is also applied out to the surrounding fields.

The land is responsible for producing the food and livelihood for Cather's characters. It is the feminine, nurturing Earth Mother. In contrast, then, those that prey upon the earth are set up in the masculine role. This is not just limited to animals and humanity as a species, although Cather does make full use of the snake to represent male dominance. Another symbol that she employs is that of the plow. The plow is made of hard metal and steel, with the plowshare forming an inverted V-shape, also known as a chevron. The chevron is a traditional symbol of masculinity, which corresponds with the female V-shape, or vessel. The plowshare tills the soil, leaving a V-shaped furrow in the earth. This furrow is then filled with seed, making the earth ready to produce a new crop.

By sitting down in the middle of the garden and being sure that no snakes can "approach unseen," Jim is setting himself up as a guardian of the feminine domestic rather than an intruding force. He carries no seed, either physically or biologically considering his age, and neither does he bring any farming tools like a plow or spade into the garden. For this brief period, the landscape is devoid of any masculine machinery or interference, leaving it with what Marx calls a "strangely soft, tender feeling" because it is being protected rather than invaded.[15] It is not even in danger from mankind, for Jim is guarding it against the approach of snakes and other forms of masculinity. Lambert describes this role of the guardian as an "androgynous"

---

[12] Cather, 16.
[13] Simone de Beauvoir, "Myths: Of Women in Five Authors." In *The Critical Tradition: Classic Texts and Contemporary Trends,* ed. David H. Richter (New York: Bedford/St.Martin's, 2007), 676.
[14] de Beauvoir, 676.
[15] Leo Marx, *The Machine in the Garden: Technology and the Pastoral Ideal in America* (London: Oxford U P, 1964), 356.

male that is "supportive of female ambition."[16] It is a role that Lambert claims Cather uses often in her novels prior to *My Ántonia*. Jim understands the danger that the masculine snake holds for him and the feminine domestic and works to prevent its approach. This is furthered later when he and Ántonia visit the prairie dog town, a physical representation of the womb, and he attacks and kills a giant rattlesnake.

The adventure starts out innocently enough – as an exploration of new territory. The scene, however, is heavily laced with sexual imagery and metaphor. First, Jim states that he and Ántonia were "examining a big hole with two entrances" that "sloped into the ground at a gentle angle."[17] This opening, in the middle of a prairie dog town, represents the sexual and reproductive openings on a woman's body. The gentle slope of the ground, suggesting feminine curves, is in direct contrast to the description given of the snake, which is "thick" and muscled, with "tight coils," containing a "disgusting vitality."[18] Jim describes the opening as being "dusty from use, like a little highway over which much travel went."[19]

As a sexual description, this idea of a well-traveled road, conjures up images of the accepted female role in society as a sexual object that is only valued for her ability to reproduce. Jim marvels at the prairie dogs' abilities to create such large and deep holes, wondering how they carried the gravel up from so deep in the earth, much like a woman creates a child within the womb and must carry it out into the world from so deep within her. This concept is also reinforced by Jim's claim that the prairie-dog town is composed of a good number of holes, spread regularly apart, creating an image of the passive woman as a receptacle waiting to be filled with life.

Jim is investigating a particularly large opening with Ántonia, exploring it in a sexual way that he will never explore her body, when he encounters the large snake. Ántonia screams in fear at the appearance of the snake, a classic phallic symbol as well as a symbol of evil. The phallic-likeness of the snake is heightened by its "vitality" and the description of it being ready to "spring his length," which is reminiscent of male ejaculation.[20] The positioning of the snake at the head of the opening also offers the idea of sexual intercourse and male domination, prompting Ántonia's fearful response. The snake, as a phallic symbol, thus becomes a metaphor for the dominant male class. Cather furthers this metaphor by having the snake lay

---

[16] Lambert, 679-680.
[17] Cather, 30.
[18] Cather, 31.
[19] Cather, 30.
[20] Cather, 31.

in "loose waves, like a letter 'W'."[21] The "W" stands for the idea of "woman" that is encased in the tight coils of the male symbol.

Jim regards his response to the snake as being heroic and reminiscent of a "dragonslayer," but it actually pulls Jim out of the masculine role.[22] With the snake acting as a phallic representative, its subsequent beheading and death then becomes a scene of castration. Freud claims the fear of castration is one of the most prominent in the human psyche, particularly for males.[23] Jim's reaction to the snake and active role in its demise, however, does not denote fear for the loss of the phallic, but rather an excitement and rejoicing at the fact. Jim is fulfilling the role he set himself earlier as the guardian of the garden, protecting against the invasion of snakes.

Jim says the snake's "abominable muscularity" makes him "sick."[24] Once he attacks the snake, Jim claims his strokes with the shovel come less from a survival instinct and more from a place of loathing and hatred.[25] His violent dispatch of the phallic symbol in the tunnel does not make Jim a conquering hero, but rather works as a castration of his own manhood; Jim is now free to explore a closer relationship with Ántonia because he no longer poses a sexual threat to her. The death of the snake has taken away the fear of sexual domination between them. This castration of Jim is also seen later during his sexualized dreams about Lena when she walks towards Jim carrying a "curved reaping-hook."[26] The reaping hook would be used to cut shocks of wheat, which represent the idea of masculine sexual maturity.[27] In his dreams, Lena kisses Jim, but all the while he wishes he could have the dream about Ántonia. Jim can never be sexually interested in Ántonia because he has castrated himself through the snake and Lena's reaping-hook has finished the job.

The character of Lena also serves Cather in another way, setting up the Ave/Eve dichotomy. Gilbert and Gubar describe this character opposition as the idea that society only recognizes women in one of two ways: "women are warned that if they do not behave like angels they must be monsters."[28]

---

[21] Cather, 31.
[22] Cather, 33.
[23] Sigmund Freud, "The Uncanny," 1925. In *The Norton Anthology of Theory and Criticism*, ed. Vincent B. Leitch, (New York: W.W. Norton & Company, 2001), 938.
[24] Cather, 31.
[25] Cather, 31.
[26] Cather, 123.
[27] Blanche H. Gelfant, "The Forgotten Reaping-Hook: Sex in *My Ántonia.*" *American Literature,* 43.1 (March 1971), 66.
[28] Gilbert and Gubar, 2029.

Lena represents the angelic depiction of women. Part of her angel-like demeanor comes from her introduction to the majority of the townsfolk in Cather's novel. Lena makes her first public appearance as a sexual individual at church. She has been given a new dress and shoes by a woman of the church and when she enters, everyone is awestruck by her appearance: "The congregation stared at her. Until that morning no one [...] had realized how pretty she was, or that she was growing up."[29] Lena has matured into a young, beautiful and sexual woman, fulfilling all the societal requirements of a healthy wife.

Contrasted against her is the character of Crazy Mary. She represents the "monstrous" woman of society, responding to Lena's sexuality with violence. After watching her husband's reaction to Lena's presence, Mary chases Lena down the road, threatening to "come over with a corn knife one day and trim some of that shape off" of the younger woman.[30] Mary refuses to exist within the set boundaries of society and, as such, is considered crazy by her husband and the townsfolk. She also represents, once again, the feeling of illness Gilbert and Gubar claim women experience when trying to assimilate into patriarchal society. Cather also makes use of her as a warning to that same male dominated society. One day, Mary chases Lena to the Shimerdas with a corn knife in her hand. She makes Jim and Ántonia "feel how sharp her blade was, showing [them] very graphically just what she meant to do to Lena."[31] By having Jim feel the edge of the blade, Cather reinforces the fact that Jim has been emasculated as well as showing that the women of society are, to whatever extent, armed and prepared to fight their way out from under the male dominated idea of what roles women should serve in society.

Aside from having Jim physically handle instruments of castration – Mary's corn knife and the spade that he uses on the snake - it is in Jim's dreams that Cather shows the completeness of Jim's psychological transformation into an emasculated male. Just before Jim describes his dream of Lena with her reaping-hook, he discusses a separate dream that he has about Ántonia. In this dream, he and Ántonia are running through stacks of harvested grain, climbing the stacks and "slipping down the smooth sides [...] into soft piles of chaff."[32] Just like the dream with Lena, the element of the natural world – the grain – is useless as a sexual image of reproduction. In this dream, the grain is already harvested and packed away. It has been

---

[29] Cather, 93.
[30] Cather, 93.
[31] Cather, 94.
[32] Cather, 123.

cut down and reaped by someone else, meaning that Jim has no reproductive purpose within the dream.

Secondly, Jim says they slide down into "soft piles of chaff." Chaff is worthless. It is the split and damaged seed coverings and other debris that are separated from the precious grain during threshing. Like the violence of the snake's death, the threshing machine violently cuts away the seed coverings and makes them useless. Since Jim has already been castrated, at least in a psychological sense, his own seed is useless, as well. He can never reproduce with Ántonia, or with anyone, as demonstrated by his frustrated dreams of Lena. Also, he describes the piles of chaff as being "soft," bringing up images of flaccidity and impotence.

Moving out of his dreams and the idea of psychological castration, Cather pulls in a separate hyper-sexual metaphor to describe Jim's physical emasculation. This new metaphor comes in the form of the über-male character, Wick Cutter, who is described as having a "pink, bald head" with "yellow whiskers, always soft and glistening."[33] Cather's description of Cutter is extremely phallic. Even his name, Wick Cutter, carries connotations of emasculation, castration and defloration.[34] Cutter is also said to brush his whiskers "every night, as a woman does her hair," conjuring images of masturbation and sexual potency because he is able to fulfill his duties "every night."[35] Jim "detests" Cutter, shying away from this ultimate phallic representation because it reminds him of his own emasculation and inability to explore a sexual relationship with either Lena or Ántonia.[36]

Cutter's role in Jim's castration is not just as a physical representation of the strong, sexual male potency that Jim will never achieve himself. He also takes a strong physical role in emasculating Jim, even if it is by accident and a case of mistaken identity. Ántonia, while working as a hired girl in town, rents a room from Cutter and his wife. One night, she asks Jim to sleep in her room while she stays elsewhere because she feels uncomfortable in Cutter's presence. This is the only way in which Jim is actually able to sleep with Ántonia because he has already been castrated in her eyes with the death of the snake. Also, once again, Jim has placed himself in the position of the guardian of the feminine domestic, just as he did at the start of the novel by sitting in the garden. While Jim is sleeping in her room, Cutter enters and sits down on the bed. Jim, thinking the intruder is a burglar, opts

---

[33] Cather, 115.
[34] Shaw, 536.
[35] Cather, 115.
[36] Cather, 115.

for a more passive response than an active, masculine one, choosing to "not move," hoping that Cutter would "get out without troubling [him]."[37] Because Jim does not respond with violence or action, Cutter has no reason to doubt that it is Ántonia in the bed. He sees her passivity as the acceptable feminine response to his dominating masculine presence. As such, he proceeds with his sexual advance. Jim, "threatened by unleashed male sex – the ultimate threat – he [Jim] fights with primordial violence, though again sickened with disgust."[38] Every time that Jim is faced with examples of male sexual power, he becomes sickened by it. This is evident not only during Cutter's attempted rape but also his self-castration with the snake. This sickness and disgust only come during encounters with masculine sexuality, however, as opposed to Gelfant's argument that Cather is rejecting all forms of sexuality. Part of Jim's response to masculinity may be found in Julia Kristeva's concept of abjection. Kristeva claims that "the abject has only one quality of the object – that of being opposed to *I*."[39] Having been emasculated, Jim, as the object, recognizes the sexual male power as something that is now outside of him – it has been abjected by him. As the object, Jim is in direct opposition to the abjected male sexuality and reviles coming into contact with it.

When Jim begins to fight back, Cutter becomes enraged, "choking [Jim] with one fist and beating [him] in the face with the other."[40] Cutter's response at the presence of a possible male sexual threat is primal and animalistic. He attacks Jim physically and mentally, shouting out abuses and threats not only to Jim but also Ántonia, working to defend what he sees as his rightful place as the dominant force within his sphere of power. However, because Ántonia has been removed from that sphere and Jim has taken her place, the mechanics of Cutter's power has shifted. In defining power and its relation to sex, Foucault claims that "power must be understood [...] as the multiplicity of force relations immanent in the sphere in which they operate."[41] As such, power is limited. It cannot "produce" or reproduce its own resources and is incapable of intervening in matters outside its own sphere.[42] To remove a system of power from its designated sphere would be to destroy it. Likewise, removing the object which power dominates from that sphere, removes it beyond the limits of power.

---

[37] Cather, 134.
[38] Gelfant, 70.
[39] Julia Kristeva, *Powers of Horror: An Essay on Abjection,* Trans. Leon S. Roudiez. (New York: Columbia U P, 1982), 1.
[40] Cather, 134.
[41] Foucault, 92.
[42] Foucault, 85.

It is only through this offsetting of the balance of power that Jim is able to escape Cutter's attack. Jim forces Cutter's hand away from his throat and dives out the window, running away from the stronger, more dominant male force. After returning home, the physicality of Jim's castration is seen when he looks in a mirror, noting that "truly, I [Jim] was a battered object. [...] My lip was cut and stood out like a snout. My nose looked like a big blue plum, and one eye was swollen shut and hideously discoloured (*sic*)."[43] This relates directly back to Freud's castration theory because he relates the fear of injury to the eyes to the "dread of being castrated."[44] Freud's connection between these two seemingly separate fears stems largely from the Greek tragedy of Oedipus Rex. "The self-blinding of the mythical criminal, Oedipus," Freud claims is "simply a mitigated form of the punishment of castration."[45] Through the damage to his eyes, Jim experiences a physical loss of his masculine sexuality.

After his near rape and brutal beating at the hands of Cutter, Jim resorts to hiding in his room, refusing to see anyone or tell anyone about his humiliation. When he arrives home, he pulls a shawl around him and lies down on the parlor sofa to sleep. His grandmother, who fittingly enough was the first one to warn him about the dangers of snakes – masculine sexuality – and the necessity of always keeping a weapon handy for defending oneself against them, is the one to tend to Jim's injuries. She insists on going for a doctor, but he begs her not to, saying "I could stand anything [...] so long as nobody saw me or knew what had happened to me."[46] This reaction is typical to the psychological response of most women when they encounter sexual violence such as rape or molestation. When he refuses visitors, asking only to be left alone in his room, his grandmother seems to understand.[47] She accepts his new status and does not try to force him back into the masculine realm but rather allows him to remain within the domestic sphere of the home. His transformation from an androgynous protector in the garden to an emasculated and castrated figure within patriarchal society is complete.

As for Cutter, he escapes from town, broken and bruised. As a final admonition from Cutter's tale, Cather re-introduces Cutter's wife, letting her make the threat that "Mr. Cutter will pay for this [...] He will pay!"[48] While part of this payment will no doubt be in the form of physical

---

43 Cather, 135
44 Freud, 938.
45 Freud, 938.
46 Cather, 135.
47 Cather, 135.
48 Cather, 137.

retribution from Mrs. Cutter, herself, Cutter has already been forced to pay certain dues by running away in the early light of dawn. The depot agent describes his face as being "striped with court-plaster," and his left arm is bound in a sling.[49] While it is not specifically mentioned whether Cutter has received damage to his eyes, his face, the public image of himself in society, has been damaged. He has been removed from his sphere of power and lost his social standing in the community. Cutter has no choice but to leave the town and attempt to establish himself in another space where the knowledge behind his injuries is unknown. It is not even the fact that he was attempting to force himself sexually on a woman that causes him to have to leave. Cutter must evacuate his known social sphere and move elsewhere because he, a towering symbol of masculinity, has experienced his own form of emasculation through his defeat at the hands of Jim, a weaker individual.

Besides providing a warning to the patriarchal society that Cather was trying to survive in as a woman and an artist, Cutter and the snake also serve as a call to women to challenge that same patriarchal society and their conventional place within it. With Cutter, the ruling order is challenged through the fact that Ántonia makes the active decision to not stay in the house on the night of Cutter's attack. In doing so, she has stepped outside the norm of accepted behavior. Also, Mrs. Cutter's vehement assertion of making her husband pay for his actions also presents an idea that she is more in control of their relationship than he is. He feels the need to be duplicitous and deceitful in order to follow his urges rather than just going at them straight on as would be expected by the force of greater power. In Cutter's relationship, Cather attacks the idea of female subservience within their expected social roles.

With the snake, however, Cather is attacking the patriarchy on a much more base and primal level. In describing the snake, Jim says it was "old, and had led too easy a life," referring to the long tradition of male dominated society.[50] The snake's life is complacent and uncomplicated, with his every need being met easily and without effort. He has a "sheltered home" and an "owl-feather bed," conjuring images of luxury and power[51] The fact that he can have a "fat prairie dog for breakfast whenever he felt like it" not only applies to the idea of being fed and catered to, but the prairie dog, with its hole, brings back the idea of the female being under the male's constant control.

Being able to "have" a prairie dog whenever he wants reinforces the idea that women are not independent souls but sexual and reproductive servants.

---

[49] Cather, 136.
[50] Cather, 33.
[51] Cather, 33.

The problem that Cather hits upon is that the snake "had forgot that the world doesn't owe rattlers a living."[52] Cather not only uses this as Jim's point of success in his battle with the snake but also as her main argument against patriarchal society. The complacent lifestyle of the snake makes him easier to kill, just as the complacency of men in society makes them more susceptible to attack. Cather's focus on the idea of creation in the prairie-dog town and even her so-called betrayal of Ántonia by making her a fertile object, producing ten children, shows the equal responsibility on both sexes for the survival of mankind, a concept reinforced by Simone de Beauvoir's essay, "Myths: Of Women in Five Authors." She describes the "sole earthly destiny" of women, in all incarnations, the "equal, the woman-child, the soul-sister, the woman-sex, the woman-animal" as always being man.[53] Without women, society would crumble. The novel itself works as an example of that because, without the presence of Ántonia, Jim's memories have no substance.

"Whatever ego may seek himself through her," says de Beauvoir, "he can find himself only if she is willing to act as his crucible."[54] By removing strong female characters from her later novels, Cather has removed them beyond the limits of masculine power, refusing to allow them to "act as [man's] crucible." At the same time, she embraces what Virginia Woolf would later refer to as the angel in the house, letting Ántonia end as an exultation rather than a destruction of this character. Ántonia is a married woman and the mother of ten children. She is the ultimate wife and mother, fulfilling all the roles as set down for her by society. However, she does not claim that these roles are what define her in society. During one of her last meetings with Jim, Ántonia exclaims that she "can't wait till [her] little girl's old enough to tell her about all the things" she and Jim used to do.[55] Rather than being ashamed of her upbringing, which was hardly feminine, she is eager to share with her daughter the limits of her exploits and her adventures as a strong woman. Her role as the angel in the house allows her the freedom to work within the patriarchal society to teach her daughter how to grow beyond what society says she should aspire to.

One of the most powerful images of challenge and caution toward the patriarchy within Cather's novel comes at the end of Book II, "The Hired Girls." Jim and Ántonia are talking outside when they notice a striking image in the distance:

---

[52] Cather, 33.
[53] de Beauvoir, 677.
[54] de Beauvoir, 677.
[55] Cather, 171.

On some upland farm, a plough had been left standing in the field. The sun
was sinking just behind it. Magnified across the distance by the horizontal
light, it stood out against the sun, was exactly contained within the circle of
the disk; the handles, the tongue, the share – black against the molten red.
There it was, heroic in size, a picture writing on the sun. Even while we
whispered about it, our vision disappeared; the ball dropped and dropped
until the red tip went beneath the earth. The fields below us were dark, the
sky was growing pale, and that forgotten plough had sunk back to its own
littleness somewhere on the prairie.[56]

Cather's entire message and warning to patriarchal society can be found
within this paragraph. The plough, the symbol of masculinity and industrial
power, is shown "exactly contained within the circle of the disk [the sun], a
representation of Foucault's sphere of power and influence. It has been left
out in the field, 'forgotten.'" Even though it still retains some vestiges of
power, seemingly "writing on the sun" and standing dominant above the
prairies, "heroic in size," it serves more as a symbol of the end of the era of
masculine dominance. The plough, a tool meant to be used, is left stationary
– it has no motion. Left on its own, it will rust and become useless. The sun,
which has illuminated the plough, is slowly sinking behind it, bringing
darkness. The plough stands out against the sun as a black object, signifying
death. Against the vastness of the prairies, the plough, and as such, mankind,
has been reduced to its "own littleness" once again. Within the darkness, the
plough is lost, and all the remains is the feminine landscape, the garden, the
power of rebirth and growth. From within this darkness rests the possibility
of the sun rising on a new age of power, one in which women have a better
chance of being considered equals within male dominated society.

The initial scene with the snake ends with Jim claiming that part of his
success in killing it stems from having Ántonia beside him.[57] This simple
fact, the idea of safety in numbers, works as a call to women in society to
not abandon each other, just as Cather is not abandoning women in her
novels. In creating mostly male storylines, with male characters, Cather
insinuates herself within the power-sphere of masculinity, thereby giving
herself the ability to affect the mechanics of masculine power in society. It
is not that she is discarding or deserting her role as a woman in society by
ignoring female characters in her later novels, but that she is merely finding
a new method of attack. It is through this lack of strong female characters,
this narrative blank space of femininity, that Cather can criticize the
patriarchal society because she is hiding in plain sight behind a male voice

---

[56] Cather, 133.
[57] Cather, 33.

and stereotypical female characters. Through male characters, she becomes a dragon slayer in her own right, capable of beheading the snake of male control within society, effectively castrating those who would strive to keep her down in the feminine domestic realm instead of letting her crawl above ground and enjoy the light of the rising sun.

Bibliography

Cather, Willa. *My Ántonia*, (New York: Oxford University Press, 2006).

de Beauvoir, Simone. "Myths: Of Women in Five Authors." In *The Critical Tradition: Classic Texts and Contemporary Trends,* edited by David H. Richter, 676-678. (New York: Bedford/St.Martin's, 2007).

Foucault, Michel. *The History of Sexuality: An Introduction. Vol. I.* Translated by Robert Hurley. New York: Vintage Books, 1990.

Freud, Sigmund. "The Uncanny." 1925. In *The Norton Anthology of Theory and Criticism*, edited by Vincent B. Leitch, 929-952. (New York: W.W. Norton & Company, 2001).

Gelfant, Blanche H. "The Forgotten Reaping-Hook: Sex in *My Ántonia.*" *American Literature,* 43.1 (March 1971): 60-82.

Gilbert, Sandra M. and Susan Gubar. *The Madwoman in the Attic: The Woman Writer and the Nineteenth-Century Literary Imagination.* In *The Norton Anthology of Theory and Criticism*, edited by Vincent B. Leitch, 2023-2035. (New York: W.W. Norton & Company, 2001).

Kristeva, Julia. *Powers of Horror: An Essay on Abjection.* Translated by Leon S. Roudiez. New York: Columbia U P, 1982.

Lambert, Deborah G. "The Defeat of a Hero: Autonomy and Sexuality in *My Ántonia.*" *American Literature,* 53.4 (January 1982): 676-690.

Martin, Terence. "The Drama of Memory in *My Ántonia.*" *PMLA*, 84.2 (March 1969): 304-311.

Marx, Leo. 1964. *The Machine in the Garden: Technology and the Pastoral Ideal in America.* London: Oxford U P.

Shaw, Patrick W. "*My Ántonia:* Emergence and Authorial Revelations." *American Literature* 56.4 (December 1984): 527-40.

CHAPTER NINE

DIVINITY OF NATURE:
A STUDY OF ENVIRONMENTAL ETHICS
IN MAMANG DAI'S WORKS

RASHMI ATTRI

"All healing comes from the earth. Plants not only have healing powers, but they communicate with us [...] the spirit of the earth and the land...is central to our understanding of the world and our well-being as Indigenous people [...] land is the foundation of everything for [Indigenous people] now and into the future."[1]

The quote above finds best expression in the lifestyle of tribal communities of Northeast states of India, which even in modern industrial times with rampant destruction try to retain oneness with nature. Respect and regard for nature has been an important aspect of the lives of the tribal communities of India. One such tribe is the Adi tribe of Arunachal Pradesh of Northeast Indian state, which has mythical links with different forms of nature. In fact, nature plays a very important role in their rituals and festivals. The biophysical, the physical, and supernatural worlds are bound together. Their environmental ethics takes exception to anthropocentric worldviews wherein man has the power to control nature.

The northeast region of India consists of seven states known as seven sisters, namely: Assam, Nagaland, Manipur, Mizoram, Tripura, Sikkim, and Arunachal Pradesh. The northeast region is extraordinarily diverse and rich in natural resources, beauty, and in its people's rich social and cultural heritage. The tribal people of these states do not share common history or heritage. Issues related to ethnicity and identity are important for them and writers have also written about these issues. Socio-cultural life finds

---

[1] Kailash C. Baral, "Articulating Marginality: Emerging Literatures from Northeast India," Emerging Literatures of Northeast India: The Dynamics of Culture, Society, and Identity (New Delhi: Sage Publication India Pvt Ltd, 2013) 114-116

expression in the writings coming from these regions and thus asserting their racial and ethnic identities. About the origin of tribes in these states Mamang Dai comments:

> ...origin is still shrouded in mystery. No conclusive data about their early history and progress of grants has been ascertained. It is however believed that they came from the triangle of Burma, where numbers of magnolia tribal groups of similar culture lived in a widely dispersed area between the Salween, Makong, and Yangtze rivers...among the Adi it is presumed that their original home was somewhere in Tibet...it is not clear as to what events impelled them to leave their original home.[2]

Arunachal Pradesh, (one of the world's 25 biodiversity hotspots), showcases in the present narrative as a profoundly mysterious and magical zone of ecology: "Nature has been bountiful to Arunachal Pradesh. The Himalayan region captures some of the heaviest rain falls and the result is an expanse of lush tropical forests where life breeds in myriad forms... where life sustains itself in a delicate balance that is vulnerable to extinction by even the smallest threat to the habitat."[3] In Sanskrit language, the name Arunachal Pradesh means, "The land of dawn lit mountains." Describing the state like a conscious historian, the author informs that this region has 26 tribes with over one hundred and ten sub clans each with a different language and dialect. Dai further says:

> In terms of its unique cultural variety, scenic beauty and unexplored ecological wealth, Arunachal Pradesh remains, 'til today, a last great frontier of traditional culture. The state is a rich storehouse of medicinal and economically potential species. There are about 200 medicinal plant species which are used by the tribes [...] the land is criss-crossed by rivers and high mountain ranges running north south that divide it into five river valleys [...] and its relay is a beautiful landscape.[4]

This paper seeks to explore the environmental ethics of the Adi tribe of Arunachal Pradesh, India with reference to Mamang Dai's fictional works namely, *The Legends of Pensam,* while making passing reference to her other novel, *The Black Hill.* This paper with a hermeneutic and analytic approach endeavors to place the texts in the social practice and vibrant

---

[2] Mamang Dai, *The Hidden Land,* 18,20
[3] Mamang Dai, *The Legends of Pensam* (New Delhi: Penguin, 2006), Author's Note, xii
[4] Mamang Dai, *Arunachal Pradesh: The Hidden Land* (New Delhi: The Sky Prints 2009), 15

indigenous culture of the Adi tribe. Mamang Dai is a versatile writer and journalist from Arunachal Pradesh who has three novels: *The Legends of Pensam*, *The Stupid Cupid*, and *The Black Hill*, four collections of poetry, and two nonfiction books to her credit. She is not only the recipient of prestigious literary awards but has also worked with the worldwide fund for the protection of nature under the Eastern Himalaya Biodiversity hotspots programme.

The Legends of Pensam serves as the chronicle of the cultural life of the Adi tribe and is woven around their traditional and cultural belief system, since for these tribes "culture is the way of life." To quote Kailash C. Baral, "[...] in the absence of authentic histories of most communities in Northeast, the creative writers have taken it upon themselves to be cultural historians. Their works provide us the resource for writing alternative histories."[5] This narrative tells the alternative tribal history with a native spirit and can be called "ethnographic" for its vivid portrayal of ritualistic, religious, and social practices of the Adi people. The Adi tribe is one of the sub-groups of Tani people of Arunachal Pradesh.

Mamang Dai, skillfully fusing myth, tradition, memory, and fiction together, traces the mythical links of the Adi tribe with the Himalayas and nature, which provide the backdrop to her writings. Dai, herself being from the Adi tribe, brings her personal knowledge of the primitive customs and beliefs of the area. Throughout the narrative she vividly depicts the strong bond that tribes people enjoy with nature and their primitive traditions. Referring to their involvement with the outside world of nature, Dai writes in one of her articles entitled: "The Nature of Faith and Worship Among the Adi's," that "the great forest, the mountains, and the environment shaped the consciousness of the Adi people and made them decorate the Pator gate, (the gate made of leaves and branches and considered holy), with arrows tipped with ginger and the sacred branches of the Taan tree to consecrate it against evil forces."[6] In the beginning of the narratives, the author takes the readers to the beautiful upland Siang valley of the Adi's with dense forests and its beautiful rivers, mountains and rains. She writes, "Travelling the distant village still entails cumbersome river crossings, elephant rides through thick forests and over high mountain passes [...] so far, isolation has been the best protection for the pristine forest and rich biodiversity of

---

[5] Kailash C Baral, "Articulating Marginality: Emerging literatures from Northeast India" *Emerging Literatures of Northeast India: The Dynamics of Culture, Society, and Identity* (New Delhi: Sage Publication India Pvt Ltd, 2013), 8

[6] Mamang Dai, "The Nature of Faith Among the Adi," *Understanding Tribal Religion* (New Delhi: Mittal Publications 2004)

Arunachal Pradesh."[7] Further celebrating the pristine, divine unexplored wilderness, Dai writes:

> In dreams, my people say they see the rain mother sitting on the
> Treetops, laughing in the mist Her silver ornaments clink as she rides the
> wind, brandishing her sword
> Every time she twirls her skirt, the storm clouds edged with black
> Rush up to cover her.[7]

As regards to its theme, the narrative spreads across the colonial and contemporary post-colonial times, and is wide ranging as it has stories dealing with the origin of the world, history of clans, traditional beliefs, world of spirits, the entry of the British people, etc. It glorifies the pristine nature but towards the end the narrative also laments and decries the fast modernization taking place in their land. *The Legends of Pensam* is a collection of nineteen stories of three generations divided into four parts where the storytelling mode, (which is compatible with the oral tradition of the Adi tribe), is intentionally used to re-create the historical, legendary, and mythical past of the Adi tribe, which is still alive. Its four sections are titled: *Diary of the World, Song of the Rhapsodist, Daughter of the Village,* and *A Matter of Time.* Such stories as *Songs of Rhapsodists,* highlight these storytelling traditions. These stories, defying all logic, are open-ended which are not just narrated but sung and danced as in the Ponung dance where myth and story would be reborn in their song. In this manner, their traditions, customs, and beliefs are passed onto the next generations of youngsters.

Interestingly, these stories, though complete in themselves, are interconnected as they have travelled through the generations of the Adi tribe. In fact, the history of this tribe is circular. There are many stories linking the clan, and sometimes they forget how these connections were made, but everything is interconnected. The stories explain and observe the behaviour of natural phenomena and imbue them with sense and order. The book informs that the clan's root is oratory. Interspersed in all this is the larger message of environmental consciousness which forms the theme of these stories. In the very beginning, the narrative points out how man and other species came together when the author narrates the origin of their tribe: "The beginning it was nothingness. It was neither darkness nor light [...] The spark grew into the shining stream that was the consciousness of man, and from this all the stories of the world and all its creatures came into

---

[7] Dai, Forward, xii

being."[8] Indigenous psychologists also emphasize the importance of storytelling in indigenous societies. Pointing out the significance of these stories in the modern fast paced world the author comments, "We are today as members of a community belonging to a particular place with a set of beliefs and faith. It is here that we find that peculiar indefinable something by which we recognize each other and make others see us as a group, a society, a particular community."[9] [10]

An interesting thing about the book is that here we do not have a traditional, singular protagonist; rather the entire community of the Adi tribe is the focus. The word "Pensame" means "in between," suggesting the middle ground.[11] It really is the middle ground between myth and reality in the book. We get a graphic description of the daily life of the Adi tribe, their folktales, rituals, and festivals. This might sound irrational in today's scientific world, but the storyteller highlights their significance, their agricultural practices, their world of legends, myths, and stories, surrounded with dense forests, rivers, and mountains. The people of Adi tribe claim their origin to Mother Nature and their entire life—right from birth to death—is heavily dependent on nature's bounty, which forms the backbone of their cultural and religious life. We can say the land is all that they have and need, for they are spiritually related to it. The divine is pervading everywhere; it is in anything and everything. They are punished or rewarded as per their acts by these spirits. The author talks about the influence of the spirits on the tribe people and says that it is their firm faith that in the winters ghosts and spirits walk near the riverbank and watch the forest's dwellers jealously. To appease these spirits and ghosts, they call shamans to offer rituals. They believe that their tribe is constantly being scrutinized by the spirits of the land: "They understand that it was a nebulous zone that divides the worlds of spirit and man—in fact at one time man and spirits had been brothers."[12]

It is this world of spirits, deities and ghosts which protect, sustain, and punish them for their good and bad deeds. While some spirits are kind, some are rude and might haunt them if their forefathers failed to appease them through certain rituals. The author describes how Togum, one of the characters, had to perform the serpent ritual believing that the spirits of the snake had entered the body of his son which caused ailment to the child.

---

[8] Dai, Ibid, 56
[9] Mamang Dai, "Oral Narratives and Myth" *Glimpses from the Northeast*, (New Delhi: National Knowledge Commission 2009) 5-6
[10] Dai, *The Legends of Pensam*, 33
[11] Dai, *The Legends of Pensam*, vii.
[12] Dai, *The Legends of Pensam*, 33

Most of the Adi people follow, "The almighty Donyi-Polo." Regarding its significance to Adi people, Dai writes, "The traditional belief of the Adi community to which I belong is full of this union [between man and nature]. Everything has life—rocks, stones, trees, rivers, hills, and all life is sacred. This is called Donyi-polo, literally meaning Donyi-sun and Polo-moon as the physical manifestation of the supreme deity, or what I like to interpret as 'world spirit.'"[13] Like deep ecology, their pagan faith dictates that all natural objects such as plants, forests, and water bodies have living souls and all being the manifestation of the same Brahma, divine soul deserve to be worshipped. This "Donyo-polo faith is an attempt to give meaning to life through intellectual and ideological pursuits based on nature."[14] Nature is regarded as a divine gift by the Adi tribe people. Their animistic faith, "[...] which they practice is woven around forest ecology and co-existence with the natural world."[15]

As per the Adi belief system, there are many deities and spirits watching their actions. Such natural objects as the sun, moon, hills, and rivers are all possessed by spirits. In order to appease these spirits, tribe people perform various rituals. Sarit K. Chaudhary in his study on the tribes of Arunachal Pradesh comments:

> Most of the tribes believe that the forest is the abode of their numerous gods and spirits, both benevolent and malevolent in nature. Adi tribe too has this belief that the huge tree like Rotne found in their surrounding forest is the abode of the spirit called Epom. Due to this they usually don't fell such trees[16]

Tribe people worship trees as the abode of their ancestors. To them, trees are a symbol of strength and fertility. There is reference to the felling of the trees which they repent, as says a character named Hoxo, "The Big trees were brought down. The spirits of our ancestors, who dwelt in these high and sacred places fell with the trees."[17] This is a reminder to modern men about the disastrous results of using nature as a commodity. Fire is also sacred to them and it soothes them and when a person dies, "They lit big fires in a small shack that marked the grave, a fire would be kept burning

---

[13] Dai, *The Hidden Land*

[14] Dai, *The Legends of Pensam,* 86

[15] Dai, *The Legends of Pensam,* xi

[16] Sarit K. Chaudhary, "Folk Belief and Resources Conservation: Reflections from Arunachal Pradesh" Indian *Folk Life* (2008) 4-5

[17] Dai, *The legends of Pensam,* 45

all day and night for up to a year as a ritual of cleansing and farewell."[18] They worship certain animals, which according to their pagan belief system, brings good luck for them and saves them against various dangers; so the teeth of the tiger and wild boar are worshipped as symbols of luck and success. So, animism also pleads for ecological and animal rights.

The narrative hammers out that tribe people heavily depend on nature and local surroundings for their daily needs. Their cultural, religious, political, and economic activities are highly environmentally friendly. Their food habits, their entertainment sources, house building material, interior decoration, cosmetics, medicines, and spices are all derived from the forests. In all these domains we find the overwhelming presence of nature. To quote the author, "The Adi tribe have always lived off the forests without positioning any threat to its ecosystem."[19] The cultural and religious life of Adi people is embedded in the forest; most of their rituals are associated with the forest. Even their rituals, festivals, and mythical tales and legends are also rooted in nature and the environment. For the Adis, "The best way to enjoy nature is to become part of it."[20] This place is described by Dai as the land of "Pristine forests and rich biodiversity."

The narrative also recounts their emotional connection with the animal which again shows their rich ecological practices. As we flip through the pages of this narrative, we get to know their camaraderie with animals and birds of all types. We are informed that in a traditional house it is common to hear the sound of chickens, dogs, and the squealing of pigs as they roam around their houses. For the Adi people animals are not commodities but fellow beings and they notice their mirth, power, and beauty. The following lines exemplify this point: "Suddenly his (cobra) eyes were dazzled by an iridescence that took his wreath away. It was god, it was green, it was dark amethystine and changing and shining with an indescribable beauty."[21] Animals are not just biological species but fellow beings invested with emotions, feelings, intuitiveness, and intelligence in the narrative. They are not a threat to humans in any way. The ways they are not a threat can be seen in the following lines which highlight the emotional bond that exists between the men and animals:

> The logs were still lying in the pile and the elephant had been hired for the day to move the logs to the platform above the trench where they could be marked and sawed. The workman was talking loudly and moving towards

---

[18] Ibid, 14
[19] Ibid, 28
[20] Ibid, 41
[21] Ibid, 23

the woodpile when the elephant stopped dead in its tracks. No amount of cajoling, prodding, or threats would move the beast to take another step. It dawned on the frustrated men that maybe the snake had made its home among the logs. What else would frighten a tusker standing nine feet tall and with the strength to kill them all if it wanted to.[22]

Nature in its varied forms is their identity marker. The tribe people treat nature as an extension of their own self which they respect and care for. They express their feelings to the trees, treating them as human, as their confidants. Tribe people are often compared with animals as Nenem in the text, one of the characters, who is compared to a river—constant, nurturing, and self-possessed. This echoes deep ecology which critiques human/man centric values, systems, and advocates a biometric view which invests the non-human world with value, independent of its usefulness to human beings. The religious beliefs of the Adi find expression in ceremonial events and festivities etc., which the Adi people carry out as part of their daily duty (dharma). By performing certain rituals, they pay their gratitude to the forces of nature. In doing so, they are sustaining biodiversity. For them religion, environment, and ethics are bound together. They consider it their duty to pay obedience to the forces of nature which nurtures them. Reverberating Hindu Vedic concept of *Vasudhaivakutumbakam,* meaning the entire world is one big family, the book foregrounds the equality of all that exists on earth where man is just one more species in the biological chain of being. All emanates from Brahma, the supreme power which resides in everything—this is how all is interrelated. The author is preaching eco-spirituality here.

This sense of oneness with nature and all its elements is expressed in Mamang Dai's, *The Black Hole,* by its protagonist Gimmur who envisions her union with her lover kajinsha, "The Gods are bystanders. And I am earth and Kajinsha is the sky and we have looked at each other and will look at each other like this for a million years."[23] This is an eco-spiritual worldview which in the words of Bron Taylor refers to "a sense of connection and belonging to nature."[24] *The Legends of Pensam,* further describes the role of nature in the lives of people of the Adi tribe, and informs the reader that most of their medicines are also derived from nature. Ginger is very important in their belief system, "Ginger was for protection. The wild ginger was the potent medicine against the evil spirits. A piece of ginger was tied

---

[22] Ibid, 22

[23] Mamang Dai, *The Black Hill* (New Delhi: Rupa publications, 2014) 289

[24] Bron Taylor, "Earth and Nature based Spirituality part 1: from Deep Ecology to Radical Environmentalism" (*Religion* 2001) 193

to the necks of the young children to ward off illness,"[25] tells an Adi woman. They use hornbill fat for arthritis and aches. A character named Bodak says that monkey meat is good for blood and believed to cure malaria. This is how nature nurtures and fulfils their needs. These age-old practices help preserve and sustain biodiversity. We see how religious and cultural life is heavily dependent on the bio-resources.

Dai narrates how their agricultural practices are also environmentally friendly by bringing in the discussion of shifting cultivation/jhulming and narrates that their traditional agricultural practice is rooted in their mythological past. The narrative informs that, "Every household has plots here for growing vegetables and herbs [...] they set off from home very early to work all morning, weeding, clearing, and planting."[26] Dai gives detailed and graphic description of the sowing procedure when she writes, "Everyone had set to work for the annual fencing of the fields for cultivation. It was the major operation. A vast tract of the jungle was cleared, and grass and bamboo were set ablaze. The fires burnt for many days and nights [...] the air cracked, and the burning debris covered the land with fertile ash."[27] This shifting cultivation is helpful in sustaining bio-resources. To protect this land, they fenced it with bamboo stakes.

Additionally, the author recounts that Adi people have their own system of protecting their harvest from bugs and insects. As against the modern insect killing sprays, they use burnt leaves for this purpose: "slowly the aroma of burning leaves scented the evening. A big fire was crackling in the garden. A cloud of smoke billowed out across the shrubs and the sugar cane stalk sand fanned out upwards to clear the air of bugs and insects."[28] Household ash is used to save the crop from pests and are the examples of traditional knowledge and sustainability of the environment.

The book also informs that people of Adi tribe practice organic cultivation. The narrative portrays the gathering of edible food from the forest which is the supplementary means of livelihood for the tribe people. Women usually collect the leafy vegetables, mushrooms, etc. In order to protect their grain from the rats they, "group the granaries together they built on stilts with a heavy circular piece of wood, like a wheel attached to the post. This was to keep the rats out."[29] Dai gives a detailed account of their festivals, which are based on seasonal cycles and directly related with their agricultural life and nature, describing the agricultural festival of the sowing

[25] Dai, *The Legends of Pensam,* 94
[26] Dai, *The Legends of Pensam,* 27
[27] Ibid, 182-3
[28] Ibid, 145
[29] Ibid, 147

when everyone sets to work for the annual fencing of the field: "A vast tract of land is cleared, and grass and bamboo are set ablaze. The fires burned for many days and nights [...] the burning debris covered the land with fertile land. Young men prepared wood and bamboo stakes and fenced the new field to protect them from grazing cattle and wild animal, making a line of demarcation that could run for miles."[30] Traditionally, in the evening after the fence is ready, the party of young men returned home dancing, "dressed in the costumes of warriors they kept high into the air, slashing, and whirling with swords... According to the old times this Tapu dance originated as a performance to drive away the spirits' fear that sometimes preyed on men."[31] These festivities continued for three days. Nature is part and parcel of their day-to-day life.

Dai also comments on the significance of rice which is their staple food and thus used for religious offerings. According to the mythology of Arunachal Pradesh rice is of divine origin. It is the gift of gods: "Its relevance is associate with all important rites of life, birth and death ranging from festivals and community feasts to marriage and ritual offerings."[32] Even beer made with rice is considered God's gift and the house where women make good rice beer is a lucky one.

Evoking the ecofeminist world, the author discusses the lives of these women, who have to do the hard work both inside the house and in the fields as well. The narrative stresses that the lives of these women depend on and revolve around nature: "They are in the forest all morning, cutting woods, cracking dry bamboo and piling stray branches seasoned by sun and rain into stacks to be carried back to the village. This is a daily necessity."[33] These women even love tending to nature and animals as is seen in the case of Nenem, a character in one of the stories. "To see the duck's great hunger and rejoice in her performance and release [...] the green of living! The young shoots of plants, the sun and the dew. The living mud, stirring of worms."[34] Here we see nature is the extension of her own self. Plants are the primary producers of food on which all animals and humankind depend. The book foregrounds the close kinship that women share with plants and animals.

Women play an important role in the preservation of the flora and fauna of the place as they spend their entire life tending to the various plants, trees, and animals. Their long contact with nature has imparted them deep

---

[30] Ibid, 182-3
[31] Ibid, 182-3
[32] Dai, *Glimpses of North East*, 7
[33] Ibid, 73
[34] Ibid, 112

knowledge about nature. Not just this, Adi women are credited with the knowledge of the medicinal value of various plants and animals which surround them. They can distinguish between the edible and non-edible plants. They know the nutrient value of various plants. The common ailments of fever, cough, and dysentery are treated by using certain herbs obtained from the local forests. These women know that "The meat of monkey is good for the blood [...] it was believed to cure malaria."[35] They are not only compatible with their surroundings but very humane; thus, Dai unravels the indigenous knowledge system of the tribe people.

The narrative also talks about the local administrative system called Kebang which plays a very crucial role in all spheres of the life of the Adi's. Describing the jurisdiction of the local administrative system, Dai notes that kebang, "functions as traditional judiciary, a council of men to take over and assemble under the tree to distil words, to explore human psychology and weigh and measure right against the wrong in the long exercise of logic and compassion."[36] Kebang also controls the use of bio- resources. Kebang does not permit the modern means of fishing is not allowed, and violation of law entails a fine of Rs 5000 and 10000. Interestingly, here the forest, which sustains the Adi people and fulfils their basic daily needs also acts like a prison for the criminals who are, "banished to live like an animal in the forest for a whole month."[37] This is a nature centric system of judicial administration where they don't need to construct prisons. This further shows how they are attuned to the environment which fulfils all their needs.

The narrative refers to the community hunting and fishing as means of their livelihood which also is a source of their entertainment during festivities. In *The Strange Case of Kalen,* the Hunter talks about community hunting and the ritual of the Kiruk."[38] By hunting, they protect their forest and fruits from being destroyed by animals. Community hunting is used to discourage indiscriminate hunting. This also comes under the jurisdiction of kebang. We get to know that they hunt deer as, "For many days they had been staking out an area where the deer came to feed on the wild fruits that litter the forest floor."[39] However it is considered taboo among Adi people to kill certain animals such as tigers for superstitious reasons. This helps maintain biodiversity. Fishing, like agriculture, plays an important role in the economy and passing time of the Adi people, for which they have ample rivers with a variety of fish. This also supplements their diet. Again, they

---

[35] Ibid, 14
[36] Ibid, 160
[37] Ibid, 11
[38] Ibid, 13
[39] Ibid, 13

have to follow the dictates of the local administration Kebang, which allows only community fishing during the specified time in the interest of biodiversity of this region. Kebang contributes towards biodiversity and sustainability in a huge manner by laying rules, which if not obeyed require punishment. Bioresources play a role in these activities as well. In fact, the instruments for hunting and fishing are made of bamboo, cane, and wood.

In every sphere, their surrounding flora and fauna fulfil all their needs. For example, their traditional houses are described in the following lines, "Losi grew up in the house that was built in a traditional style with projecting Bamboo veranda perched on stilts."[40] Such wooden houses are the best protection against the earthquakes which often occur there. Buildings that are mostly built of bamboo are light. The interior decoration is also eco-friendly as its the material available there. Mostly the skull of Methuen's and the jaws of pigs are used to decorate their houses. Flooring is done with the bamboo sheets and the pillars of which the houses are erected, are again made of logs. All of this is available from the jungles they live in.

Since the Adi people are portrayed in absolute sync with their external natural world, they don't have concrete boundaries, and it is the trees which serve this purpose as is described, "Duyang group of villages clustered together in the middle of cane thickets and clumps of bamboo [...] the villages ran into each other and only a tree, a rock, or narrow stream cutting across the path marked the loose boundaries."[41] This is the perfect example of a simple, rustic, pristine, sylvan setting where except for the rich flora and fauna nothing is needed to survive.

The death rituals of the Adi people are also rooted in nature. This is pointed out in the story, *The Homecoming,* which tells that the mother of the narrator was buried under the big tree and the soul is crowned with the shower of sacred leaves. Hence right from their birth till they die, tribespeople live in the lap of nature fearing that the evil spirits live in the trees, it is taboo to cut trees. Their traditional belief system supports ecological bonding. In the following lines Dai informs about the non-anthropocentric cosmogenesis, "From nothingness we have come to be born under the stars, and mighty Donyi polo—the sun and the moon, whose light shines on all equally, is the invisible force that guides each one of us. All life is light and shadow: we live and we die, and the path of destiny is the quest for faith."[42]

---

[40] Ibid, 23
[41] Ibid, 74
[42] Ibid, 58

In the last part of the narrative, the author laments the rampant modernization and industrialization tracking the land which the villagers are not happy with. Dai states: "But it was not that the change had not touched our land or had come only recently. The first white priests, surveyors and soldiers had begun arriving in the region almost two hundred years ago, in the early 1800."[43] Again, in the last sections, Dai sketches the painful reality of change and writes: "The texture and speed of change was visible in strange ways all across the land."[44] Even nature is moaning at this commercialization when "The tree made an indescribable sound as it fell as if the old tree was weeping."[45] The author laments, "the rape of mother nature by the industrial giants."[46] Tribes people have their doubts if it is good or bad. One of the characters feel, "that we need courage and faith in the face of change,"[47] while another comments, "this is your land. Whatever happens there is nothing to fear."[48]

What distinguishes these tribal people is their close association with the natural environment. The narrative advocates ecological vision of the essential unity of all beings for a harmonious and balanced life where there is no hierarchy between man and nature and decries the notions of development in the name of modernization. Being in harmony with the natural world leads to prosperity and well-being of all. Dai presents a society with a harmonious ecological vision where, "Every winter men from the surrounding villages perched on the highest ridges set out on a journey to mountains to harvest precious root."[49] Eco-critics, and deep ecologists, uphold this interdependence and egalitarian approach towards nature and its species. Thus, "Seeing the world as a mere object implies its exploitation; seeing it or feeling it as a mirror of the self, which is more or less an ecological position, may imply a sense of caring and living in relation to rather than excreting power over the world."[50] The Adi tribe feel like nature and environment is not outside them but part of themselves, which is meant by the Hindi word for environment, "*paryavaran*," meaning that which encircles us, surrounds us. Their ethics for biospheric egalitarianism

---

[43] Dai, *The Legends of Pensam*, 37
[44] Ibid, 188
[45] Ibid, 159
[46] Chandra and Das, 65
[47] Dai, *The legends of Pensam*, 43
[48] Ibid, 68
[49] Ibid, 58
[50] Malcolm Miles, *Eco-Aesthetics: Art, literature, and Architecture in a Period of Climate Change* (2014) 10

demands, "deep seated respect [...] for ways and forms of life."[51] So, *The Legends of Pensam* Narrates the ecological tribal history with pristine forests and rich biodiversity. Dai's focus in her works is to keep this rich biodiversity intact since it defines their life, culture, religion and physical location. The revival of the strong bond between man and nature is very important in the present times of ecological crisis. Dai's narrative echoes the basic ethos of Indian culture which is compassion and reverence towards nature.

Bibliography

Baral, Kailash C. "Articulating Marginality: Emerging Literatures from Northeast India." Emerging Literatures of Northeast India: The Dynamics of Culture, Society and Identity. Edited by Margret Ch Zama. New Delhi: Sage Publication India Pvt Ltd, 2013.

Carson, Rachel. 1964. Silent Spring. Greenwich: Fawcett Publications.

Chaudhary, Sarit K. "Folk belief and Resource Conservation: Reflections from Arunachal Pradesh." *Indian Folk life*, 4-5, 28. 2008.

Dai, Mamang, *The Legends of Pensam*. London, Penguin Books, Private Limited. New Delhi, 2006.

—. *Arunachal Pradesh: The Hidden Land*. Published by Sky prints, New Delhi, 2009.

—. "The Voice of the Mountain," India International Centre, Quarterly. Vol. No2/3 2005.

—. "The Nature of Faith among the Adi's." *Understanding Tribal Religion*, Mittal Publishes, 2004.

—. "Oral Narratives and Myth." *Glimpses from the North-East, National Knowledge Commission*, 2009.

—. *The Black Hill*. New Delhi: Rupa Publications, 2014.

—. "The Nature of Faith and Worship Among the Adis." In T. Mibang and S. K. Chaudhuri (Eds.), *Understanding Tribal Religion*, 87-94. New Delhi, India: Mittal Publications.

Hazarika, Sanjoy, Strangers *from the Mist: Tales of War and Peace from India's North East*, New Delhi: Penguin, 1995.

---

[51] Arne Naess, "The Shallow and the Deep, Long –Range Ecology Movements: A Summary In G Sessions" (*Deep Ecology for the Twenty First Century* (London Shambhala Publications 1995) 151-2

Hettinger, Ned. "Eco spirituality: First Thought", *Dialogue and Alliances*, 9. No 2. 1995. Fall-Winter. http://hettingern.people.cofc.edu/HettingerEcospirituality.pdf. pp. 81-98.

Miles Malcolm. *Eco-Aesthetics: Art, literature, and Architecture in a Period of Climate Change (Radical Aesthetics- Radical Art)* Bloomsbury Academic. 2014.

Naess, Arne. "The Shallow and the Deep, Long-Range Ecology Movements: A Summary In G Sessions." *Deep Ecology for the Twenty-First Century,* London: Shambhala Publication, 1995.

Rexlin. T. and Latha, Mercy. "Mamang Dai's The Black Hill: A Story from Border Perpetuating Borderland Consciousness". *International Journal of Recent Research Aspects*, 600-603. 2018.

Taylor, Bron. "Earth and Nature-Based Spirituality (Part I): From Deep Ecology to Radical Environmentalism."*Religion.* 31, 175-193. 2001.

CHAPTER TEN

ARE LANYER'S *EVE'S APOLOGY* (1611) AND DELONEY'S *IN PRAISE OF WOMEN* (1593) FROM THE SAME PEN?

MARK BRADBEER

In 1611, the pioneering feminist poet, Aemilia Bassano Lanyer, published an anthology of her poetry, called *Salve Deus Rex Judaeorum*. She was thus the "first Englishwoman to publish a substantial volume of original poems".[1] Out of the blue, Aemilia Lanyer, a forty-two-years old commoner woman with no known history as a poet, displayed an "unapologetic assertion of poetic vocation."[2] In addition to being a talented woman writing poetry at a time when only 5-10% of women were literate,[3] she was particularly notable for breaking several barriers for women. For example, in this one publication, we have:

(a) a woman assertive enough to publish her poetry.
(b) a woman brave enough to have the poems attributed to her.
(c) a woman brave enough to publish feminist poetry.
(d) a commoner woman having a noblewoman's support.
(e) a publisher willing to publish her poetry.
(f) censors allowing her poetry to be published.

All these elements needed to be in place before we could come to know about this extraordinary poet. She had agency, both intrinsic and extrinsic. Did these elements occur simultaneously or at different times? This chapter will suggest that some of these elements probably fell into place for Lanyer much earlier than 1611, and that she used the male allonym of Thomas

---

[1] Lewalski, "Seizing Discourses and Reinventing Genres", 49
[2] Woods, "Vocation and Authority: Born to Write", 89.
[3] Brown, *Better a Shrew than a Sheep,* 21.

Deloney. This requires knowing something of her personal signature as evident in her life and work. Let us briefly look at some of her poems.

To the Queen's Majesty is the first poem of her anthology. It addresses Queen Anne, but also alludes to the previous queen. Despite being a commoner, it suggests that she knew Queen Elizabeth:

> Since great Eliza's favour blest my youth;
> And in the confines of all cares doe dwell,
> Whose griev'd eyes no pleasure ever view'th:
> But in Christ's sufferings such sweet taste they have,
> As makes me praise pale Sorrow and the Grave.
> And this great Ladie whom I love and honour,
> And from my tender years have knowne, (lines 110-6)

This may appear to be presumptuous familiarity with Queen Elizabeth I, but it accords with reports that Lanyer's father was not just a Royal Court musician, but Princess Elizabeth Tudor's Italian and lute teacher between 1545 and 1552.[4] In 1565, Baptiste and the Queen exchanged New Year's gifts. Baptist gave the Queen two pairs of gloves in 1568, one year before Aemilia was born.[5] As John Florio wrote in His First Fruits (1578):[6]

> Hath the queen musicians?
> Yes sir, man, but they are almost all Italians
> Doth she love Italians?
> Yea sir, very well.
> Delights she to speak with them?
> Yea sir, and she speaketh very eloquently.

This familiarity could potentially give him, and his daughter of "tender years", unusual access to "great Eliza", and confirm not only the words of Aemilia Bassano Lanyer's verse, but those of her astrologer's case-book, "she hath been favoured much of her mati [Majesty]".[7]

In her poem, To the Lady Susan, Countess of Kent and daughter of the Duchess of Suffolk, Aemilia Bassano Lanyer writes about Lady Susan thus:

> Come you that were the Mistris of my youth,
> The noble guide of my ungoverned days;
> Come you that have delighted in God's truth,

---

[4] Lasocki, "Alvise Bassano", Oxford Dictionary of National Biography.
[5] Bollard, Italian Material Culture at the Tudor Court, 167.
[6] Florio, His First Fruits, EEBO image 30.
[7] Woods, "Vocation and Authority: Born to Write", 84.

Help now your handmaid to sound forth his praise:
...
And since no former gaine hath made me write,
Nor my desertlesse [i.e. undeserved] service could have wonne,
Onely your noble Virtues do incite
My Pen, they are the ground I write upon; (lines 1- 4, 43-6)

The Countess of Kent's role in her upbringing is confirmed in the case-notes of her astrologer, Simon Forman.[8] Her "handmaid" service probably occurred soon after her father, Baptist Bassano, died in 1576 when Aemilia was 7 years old.[9] As indicated by the title of the poem, Lady Susan was daughter of Catherine Bertie née Willoughby, Duchess of Suffolk.

Between the death of Susan Bertie's first husband in Reginald Grey, 5th Earl of Kent, in 1573, and her marriage to John Wingfield in 1581, Susan probably lived at her family home at Willoughby House, London, where she could mentor her young "handmaid". It is not known when Aemilia finished her "service" at Willoughby House, but it is presumed that it was there that she achieved her extensive Classical education, which she obviously possessed to publish her book, *Salve Deus Rex Judaeorum* (1611).[10] It is possible that her "handmaid" duties may have extended to Susan's aged mother, the Catherine Bertie née Willoughby, Duchess of Suffolk (1519-80) and her husband, Richard Bertie (1516-82). Catherine Bertie also was a supporter of the early women writers, Anne Askew, Katherine Parr and Anne Lock. Both Lock and the Berties fled to the Continent during Queen Mary's persecution of Protestants, and Lock's first published dedication was to Catherine Bertie.[11] Suzanne Woods has also noted that "Anne Lock's only brother and his wife were close friends of Aemilia Lanyer's parents."[12] While some scholars suspect Aemilia Bassano was at Willoughby House until the age of 13, in 1582,[13] others believe she may have been there until 1587, the year her mother died and when Aemilia was aged 18.[14]

By 1585 until 1590, there was another person at Willoughby House. While Catherine Bertie's son, Peregrine, also called Lord Willoughby, was commander of the English army on the Continent, he employed a secretary

---

[8] Barroll, "Looking for Patrons", 32.
[9] Woods, *Lanyer: A Renaissance Woman Poet*, 9.
[10] Woods, *Lanyer: A Renaissance Woman Poet*, 9.
[11] Lock, *The Sermons of John Calvin*.
[12] Woods, "Anne Lock and Aemilia Lanyer: A Tradition of Protestant Women Speaking", 171.
[13] Hudson, *Shakespeare's Dark Lady: Amelia Bassano Lanier*, 140.
[14] Woods, *The Poems of Aemilia Lanyer: Salve Deus Rex Judaeorum*, xviii.

to run his affairs from Willoughby House during the Lord's absence.[15] He was the activist Protestant writer, lawyer and propagandist, John Stubbes (c.1543-1590). The possibility that Lanyer's education included tuition from Stubbes cannot be discounted.

In this context, it may be relevant to know that many years later, Aemilia's new patron was Margaret Clifford née Russell, who resembled Susan Bertie in two interesting ways. Whereas Susan's mother was the dedicatee of Anne Lock's first work, Margaret's sister was the dedicatee of Lock's last work in 1590.[16] Secondly, like Susan's family, Margaret's father, Sir Francis Russell, had been a Marian exile, and had employed a Protestant activist secretary. He was William Page. Page and Stubbes had together published the controversial book called *The Gaping Gulf* (1579) which had outraged Queen Elizabeth for suggesting that she should not marry the Catholic Duke of Anjou. The Queen ordered their right hands to be amputated on public gallows on the 3rd of November, 1579. Many scholars believe that Stubbes and Page were not acting alone, but had the secret support of noblemen and members of parliament.[17]

In 1604, Lanyer was living at Cookeham with her patron, Margaret Clifford, and her daughter Anne Clifford.[18] Aemilia Bassano Lanyer appeared to be employed as "some sort of music tutor, though she may also have helped Anne with French and Italian".[19] In her poem, *The Description of Cookeham* (lines 160-2), these three people are referred to by different names.

The daughter, Anne, is referred to as "Dorset" (lines 119 & 160). This indicates that the poem was completed after the 27th of February, 1609, when Anne married Richard Sackville Earl of Dorset. In this poem, Aemilia Lanyer remembers Margaret and her young daughter in the Cookeham garden, and the creatures there: –

> Giving great charge to noble memory,
> There to preserve their love continually:
> But specially the love of that fair tree,
> That first and last you did vouchsafe to see:
> In which it pleas'd you oft to take the ayre,
> With noble Dorset, then a virgin faire;
> Where many a learned book was read and scann'd

---

[15] Hasler, P.W. (ed.), *History of Parliament* under "John Stubbe (c.1543-90)".
[16] Lock, *Of the Marks of the Children of God.*
[17] Lake, "The Politics of Popularity", 74-6
[18] Malay, "Positioning Patronage: Lanyer's *Salve Deus Rex Judæorum* and the Countess of Cumberland in Time and Place," 251-264.
[19] Woods, *Lanyer: A Renaissance Woman Poet,* 30.

To this faire tree, taking me by the hand,
You did repeat the pleasures which had past,
Seeming to grieve they could no longer last.

These verses indicate Aemilia's role, in 1604, as reading tutor to the 14-years old "virgin-fair" daughter, Anne, and her intimacy with the Anne's mother, the noblewoman, Margaret Clifford, Countess of Cumberland.

In Lanyer's poem, Margaret Clifford is referred to by the italicised name, *Phoenix*. Aemilia also twice refers to a person with the italicized name, *Philomel* (lines 31 & 189):

And *Philomela* with her sundry layes (line 31)
Faire *Philomela* leaves her mournful Ditty (line 189)

The italicized *Philomela* appears to be self-referential, Lanyer being the poet of her patron. It is also an intimation of Aemilia's difficult past. As revealed in her astrologer's records, she had a history of being sexually abused, about which she could not freely speak. It is estimated that in 1587, the married, 65-years old Lord Hunsdon, all-powerful as Governor of the Army and cousin of the Queen, made the 18-year-old Aemilia his mistress.[20] She was subsequently made to marry Alphonse Lanyer, after she became pregnant to Hunsdon.[21] This marriage was not for love, but "for colour"; that is, to hide the Lord's adultery and wantonness.[22] Yet her astrologer notes that she cannot keep a secret, but was "brave",[23] further strengthening the parallel with Philomel who overcame her silencing.

Both the poet, Aemilia Lanyer, and her patron, Margaret Clifford, were in loveless relationships with husbands who squandered their wealth.[24] Both women had little say in the choice of husband and lived in a society in which women were systemically dependent upon men.

In a prose preface to her poem, *Salve Deus Rex Judaeorum* titled, *To the Vertuous Reader*, Aemilia lamented the misogyny of:

evil disposed men, who forgetting they were borne of women, nourished by women, and that if it were not by meanes of women, they would be quite

---

[20] Rowse, *The Poems of Shakespeare's Dark Lady*, 14, and Woods, *Lanyer: A Renaissance Woman Poet*, 16.
[21] Woods, *The Poems of Aemilia Lanyer: Salve Deus Rex Judaeorum*, xviii.
[22] Benson, "To Play the Man: Aemilia Lanyer and the Acquisition of Patronage", 416.
[23] Woods, *The Poems of Aemilia Lanyer: Salve Deus Rex Judaeorum*, xx-xxi.
[24] Lewalski, *Writing Women of Jacobean England*, 396n, and Raber, *Dramatic Difference: Gender, Class and Genre in the Early Modern Drama*, 105.

extinguished out of the world, and the final ende of them all, doe like Vipers deface the wombes wherein they were bred.[25]

An example of such evil-disposed men, is the prolific writer, Thomas Nashe, who wrote extensively against women in his *Anatomy of Absurdity, Containing a brief confutation of the slender imputed praises to feminine perfection* (1589). He challenged "women, assembling their senate, [who] will seek to stop my mouth,"[26] without mentioning that his secret patrons were the press censors, John Whitgift, Archbishop of Canterbury and Richard Bancroft, Bishop of London.[27] This publication was later followed with Nashe's sanctimonious and hypocritical *Christ's Tears Over Jerusalem* (1593), under the patronage of Lord Hunsdon's family. In it he also attacked women for men's vices, using the theological argument about Eve's sin in the Garden of Eden:

> Ever since Eva was tempted, and the serpent prevailed with her, women have took upon them both the person of the tempted and the tempter. They tempt to be tempted, and not one of them, except she be tempted, but thinks herself contemptible. Unto the greatness of their great-grandmother Eva they seek to aspire, in being tempted and tempting[28]

And:

> Women, as the pains of the devils shall be doubled that go about hourly tempting, and seeking whom they may devour, so except you soon lay hold on grace, your pains in hell (above men's) shall be doubled, for millions have you tempted, millions of men (both in soul & substance) have you devoured. To you, half your husbands' damnation (as to Eva) will be imputed.[29]

Such supposed theological logic confirmed the prejudices of its time and increased their legitimacy by being printed, and supported by the episcopal press censors. Aemilia Lanyer engaged with this misogynist's argument in the theological terms utterly of their time, particularly as it coincided with the newly-minted King James Bible (1611).

The longest poem (1840 lines) in her anthology is *Salve Deus Rex Judaeorum*, after which her anthology is named. At the centre of this poem

---

[25] Rowse, *The Poems of Shakespeare's Dark Lady*, 77.

[26] Nashe, *Anatomy of Absurdity* (1589/90). EEBO image 7.

[27] McKerrow, *The Works of Thomas Nashe*, Vol.5, 48.

[28] Nashe, *Christ's Tear Over Jerusalem* (1593). EEBO image 75.

[29] Nashe, *Christ's Tear Over Jerusalem* (1593). EEBO image 77.

is the section, *Eve's Apology in Defence of Women* (lines 762-848). Prefacing
it (lines 744-760) is a paraphrase of Matthew 27:19 about the advice of
Pilate's wife:

> When he [Pilate] was set down on the judgement seat, his wife sent unto him
> [a message] saying, "Have thou nothing to do with this just man [Jesus]: for
> I have suffered many things this day in a dream because of him."

Whereas a woman defended Jesus, Pilate and the mob of men condemned
him. This is a brilliant riposte to the contemporary wisdom of the Church of
England about women. Ending the *Eve's Apology* section is the declaration
in Matthew 27: 37 about "Christ, King of the Jews" (line 848), which
somewhat evokes, in English, the poem and book's title.[30] The first of these
texts is highlighted in the initial poem of the book, *To the Queen's Majesty*:

> Behold, great Queen, fair *Eve's Apology,*
> Which I have writ in honour of your sexe,
> And do referre unto your Majesty,
> To judge if it agree not with the Text:
> And if it doe, why are poore Women blam'd,
> Or by more faultie Men so much defam'd? (lines 73-78)

Lanyer appears to be alerting the Queen to this important verse, Matthew
27:19, on behalf of women.

Eve's Apology in Defence of Women is comparable with the earlier *In
Praise of Women,* a poem in an anthology by Thomas Deloney, called *The
Garland of Good Will* (1593). This poem presents a variety of defences for
Eve and woman. The first stanza explains that Adam loved Eve, and the
third stanza describes the goodness of a virtuous wife. The fourth stanza
acknowledges that there may be some bad women, yet "nor do I know of
any she" (line 53), while the fifth stanza points out "the glory of the female
kind, I meane our Noble Queene" (lines 69-70). This is reminiscent of
Lanyer's "great Eliza" who "from my tender years have knowne", and her
appeal to Queen Anne's authority (wife of James I) in *To the Queen's
Majesty.*

Deloney's most theological defence is in the second stanza as shown in
Table 1.

---

[30] Technically, *Salve Deus Rex Judaeorum,* translates to "Hail God, King of the
Jews".

Table 1.

In Praise of Women (1593) Stanza 2 (lines 19-28)	Salve Deus Rex Judaeorum (1611) Stanza 104 (lines 825-32)
Although that <u>Eve</u> committed then so great <u>offence</u> Ere she went hence, A recompence in our <u>defence,</u> she made mankind again: For by her blessed seed, We are redeemed indeed: <u>Why should</u> not then all mortal men, esteem of women well. And love their wives even as their lives, As nature doth compel?	_Eve's Apology in <u>Defence</u> of Women_ Then let us have our Liberty again, And challenge to yourselves no Sov'reignty; You came not in the world without our pain Make that a bar against your cruelty; Your fault being greater, <u>why should</u> you disdain Our being your equals, free from tyranny? If one woman simply did <u>offend</u> This sin of yours hath no excuse, or end.

This stanza asks virtually the same question as that in _Eve's Apology_, as shown with the underlined words, "Why should...?". Deloney's alludes to Mary, mother of Jesus, who "made mankind again:/ For by her blessed seed/ we are redeemed indeed". In _Eve's Apology_, Lanyer makes a more determined and assertive theological argument, declaring that men, including Adam, should take responsibility for their own actions: "Adam cannot be excus'd, / Her fault [Eve's fault] though great, yet he was most to blame." (stanza 98). This is the antithesis of Nashe's argument in _Christ's Tears Over Jerusalem_. This is followed by stanza 104 in Lanyer's _Salve Deus Rex Judaeorum_, noting the message of Pilate's wife sent to her husband which warns him not to condemn Jesus. Pilate is deaf to her and relents to the mob of men baying for Jesus's blood. In stanza 105, Pilate's wife "speaks for all" women. Pilate's wife's advice bookends Eve's advice to Adam.

In line 21 of _In Praise of Women_, not only does the poet speak on behalf of all women, he speaks of "our defence", surely a curious slip, for it raises the question of Thomas Deloney's gender.

Thomas Deloney

The birthdate of Thomas Deloney, or T.D. as was his common assignation, is unknown. His son, Richard, was baptized at St Giles-without-Cripplegate church, beside Willoughby House, on the 16th of October, 1586. Deloney was a weaver and songwriter. With two other weavers, he publishing a letter of complaint about the practices of migrant weavers in June of 1595, addressed *To the Minister and Elders of the French Church of London*. As a result, he was briefly imprisoned in Newgate jail. And in June the following year, he again came to the attention of the authorities for another complaint in his more characteristic medium. The ballad, *On the Want of Corn* (1596), has not survived but it contained "certain vain and presumptuous matters, bringing in the Queen, speaking with her People dialogue-wise in very fond and undecent sort."[31] This presumptuous familiarity with the Queen angered authorities who issued an indictment[32]. He became a fugitive.

Perhaps as a consequence, in late 1596,[33] Nashe wrote of him in his *Have With You To Saffron Walden*:

> Thomas Deloney, the ballading silk-weaver, hath rhyme enough for all miracles, & wit to make a *Garland of Goodwill* more than the premises, with an *Epistle of Momus and Zoilus*, whereas his muse, from the first peeping forth, hath stood at livery at an alehouse wisp, never exceeding a penny a quart, day nor night, and this dear year, together with the <u>silencing of his looms, scarce that, he being constrained</u> to betake him to carded ale, whence it proceedeth that, since *Candlemas,* or his *Jig of John For The King*, <u>not one merry ditty will come from him</u>, but the *Thunderbolt Against Swearers, Repent, England, Repent,* & *The Strange Judgments Of God.*[34]

Based on the underlined phrases, Nashe seemed to think he had heard the last of Deloney and many of his ballads (noted in italics).[35] This was premature of Nashe, since Deloney published many more ballads, four

---

[31] Mann, *Deloney's Works*, ix.

[32] Mann, *Deloney's Works*, ix.

[33] Nashe mentions "the late deceased Countess of Derby", Margaret Stanley nee Clifford (d. 38th September 1596), and therefore this passage is likely referring to the June/July controversy over Deloney's ballad, *On the Want of Corn.*

[34] Nashe, Thomas, *Have With You To Saffron Walden* (1596). EEBO image 51.

[35] Apart from the *Garland of Good Will* (1593) anthology, most of these generally-religious ballads mentioned, are lost. *Repent, England Repent* may refer to the chorus of the ballad, *The Shoemaker of Jerusalem* (publ.1620).

novels and a narrative poem between 1506 and 1603 – not bad for a man whose primary living was as a London silk-weaver.[36]

Conveniently, Shakespeare's clown, William Kempe, publicized the rumour that Deloney died in 1600, under the cheeky subtitle, "To the Tune of Thomas Deloney's Epitaph":

> I was given since to understand your late general, Thomas died poorly, as ye all must do, and was honestly buried, which is much to be doubted of some of you. The quest of inquiry finding him by death acquitted of the Inditement.[37]

Authorities could now dispense with Deloney's indictment. But the scholar, Alan Nelson, suggests that Kempe was bending the truth, as Deloney's death is recorded in 1603 in the St Giles-without-Cripplegate parish register.[38] Presumably, Deloney was free from being pursued by *pursuivants* for the last three years of his life.

A look at Deloney's work tells a different story of his life. The 1912 biography of Deloney by Francis Mann begins: "The recorded facts of Deloney's life are very scanty. His earliest venture appears to have been *A Declaration made by the Archbishop of Cullen [Cologne] upon the Deed of his Marriage"* (1583). This declaration to the Pope was signed off on the 17th of January, 1583, and a copy was transported to England, translated and published in London by the 19th of March, 1583. This correspondence precipitated the Cologne War and escalated the Protestant Reformation. This publication would have required a team of people to orchestrate. Given the maiden Queen Elizabeth I's sensitivity regarding the recent collapse of her proposed marriage with the Duke of Anjou, and given that she "detested clerical marriage,"[39] noblemen and other powerful people may have preferred a commoner to risk their name on this publication. Other early work by Deloney was patriotic and nationalistic.

After 1590 (and the death of Stubbes), Deloney's output was less about general politics and is more feminine-oriented, as shown in the list of his poems and short prose by Deloney between 1583 and 1596 on Table 2.[40]

---

[36] His novels are *Jack of Newbury* (1596), *Thomas of Reading* (1597), *The Gentle Craft Parts 1* (1597) and *Part 2* (1598), and his narrative poem is *Canaan's Calamity* (1598), the discussion of which will require a longer dissertation.

[37] Kempe, *Nine Days Wonder*, EEBO image 16.

[38] Korp, "Shoemakers, Clowns, and Saints: The Narrative Afterlife of Thomas Deloney", 5.

[39] Carlson, "Clerical Marriage and the English Reformation", 1.

[40] Deloney's larger works will not be addressed in this paper.

Table 2.

Thomas Deloney's Writings, 1583-1596	'News'	'Feminine'[41]
Archbishop of Cologne's Marriage (1583)	*	
Lamentation of Beckles (1586)	*	
Song for Capture of Conspirators (1586)	*	
History of Faustus (1588)		
Queen at Tilbury (1588)	*	
Great Galleazzo & Don Pedro de Valdez (1588)	*	
Whips of the Spaniards (1588)	*	
Happy Victories of the French King.(1589)	*	
1591-5 (mainly of *Garland of Good Will*, 1593-6)		
Lamentation of Page's Wife (1591)[42]	*	*
The Lamentation of George Strangwidge (1591)	*	*
The Sorrowful Complaint of Mistris Page (1591)	*	*
Fair Lady Rosamond		*
How King Edgar was deceived		*
How Coventry was made free		*
Of the Duke of Cornwall's Daughter		*
Song of Queen Isabell		*
Banishment of Two Dukes		
Noble Acts of Arthur of the Round Table		*
Song of praise of Women		*
Song in praise of the Single Life		
Widow's Solace		*
A Gentlewoman's Complaint		*
How a Prince of England wooed ...		*
Alphonso and Ganselo		
Pastoral Song		*
Patient Grizel		*
Song of Truth and Ignorance		
Judith and Holofernes		*
Praise of the English Rose		
Maiden's Choice twixt Age and Youth		*
As I came from Walsingham		
The Winning of Cales (Cadiz, June, 1596)	*	
Edward III and the Countess		*
The Spanish Lady's Love		*
A Farewell to Love		
Lover by his Gifts thinketh to conquer Chastity		*
The Woman's Answer		*

---

[41] These songs use a woman's voice, or a positive portrait of a woman, or show the corruption of men. In the case of *Noble Acts*, it is the defeat of the rapist, Tarquin, and in *Lover by his gifts*, it is a warning to the Lady to be wary of being bought.

[42] Earliest surviving version of *Lamentation of Page's Wife* dates from 1670-80.

In a detailed study of Deloney's work, Christopher March noted that "there is no escaping the fact that we have here a man who was presuming to imitate the voices of women".[43] A number of the poems in his anthology, *Garland of Good Will*, not only have a strongly feminine perspective, but they sympathetically portray trapped women and kept courtesans in history, as shown in Table 3.

Table 3.

Deloney Ballad	King and Dates of Reign	Queen	Other Woman
King Edgar was deceived	Edgar (959-75)	Ethelflaed	Elfritha
Fair Rosamund	Henry II (1154-89)	Eleanor of Aquitaine	Rosamund
Shore's Wife	Edward IV (1461-70, 71-83)	Elizabeth Woodville	Elizabeth (Jane) Shore
Edward III & The Countess	Edward III (1327-77)	Philippa of Hainault	Countess of Salisbury
Duke of Cornwall's Daughter	Locrine (Holinshed bk.5, ch.10 & bk.2, ch.5.)	Gwendoline	Estrild

The poems indicated in Table 3 do not appear to be written to glorify kings, nor are they presented as elegies to noblemen in history. Rather, they voice a sympathy for women who were in positions not unlike that which the young Aemilia Bassano found herself. Deloney's *Lamentation of Master Page's Wife of Plymouth, who, being enforced by her Parents to wed him against her will...* is about a couple of lovers, Eulalia and George Strangwidge, who were executed on the 20th February, 1591.[44] The woman

---

[43] Marsh, "Best Selling Ballads and the Female Voices of Thomas Deloney", 132.
[44] This Master Page is not related to William Page.

had been forced to marry a rich old man, and she, together with her lover, arranged her husband's murder. These poems are exceptional in showing sympathy for a husband-killing wife. This sympathy is aided by an emphasis of the wife's enforced marriage. It is also not dissimilar to the enforced courtesan-roles of Rosamund, Jane Shore and Estrild mentioned above. As noted by Christopher Marsh, "no author of best-selling ballads used female voices to a comparable degree", and Deloney's "ballads may have helped women to wrestle with the problems caused by their unequal status".[45]

A Maiden's Choice betwixt Age and Youth is also an unusual topic for a poem, since it describes a young woman receiving unwanted advances from an old man. It was entered into the Stationers' Register on the 26th of August, 1591. This woman is in a peculiar situation, "like a loving wife, so I lead my life", yet declaring "Away, old man, away, thou canst not give that I require" (lines 27,28, 31, 32). She is "like" a wife, but not necessarily a wife. She longs for a youthful friend, asking him to hasten and not delay, and concluding with the challenge to the youth, "Come meet me if you dare" (line 97). This also appears to parallel Aemilia's life as a courtesan to the aged but politically powerful Lord Hunsdon, whom few men would dare cross to cuckold him of his mistress. And the historical ballads in Table 3 also have echoes of similar loss of liberty.

There are other qualities in Deloney's writings that show a perception comparable to that of Aemilia Bassano Lanyer. In 1601, Lord Willoughby died, and the following year Deloney published another anthology of poems, called *Strange Histories* (1602), containing the long ballad called *The Duchess of Suffolk's Calamity*. It again focuses on a woman, that is, Lord Willoughby's mother as she escaped from the tyranny of Queen Mary with her baby daughter, Susan, and the birth of Lord Willoughby while the Duchess was in Marian exile. Over ten years earlier, this same Lord Willoughby is praised in assisting in the *Happy Victories of the French King* (1589), translated from French by T.D., or "Thomas Deloney".[46] Having had Lord Willoughby's sister, Susan Bertie, as her "Mistris", the poet, Aemilia Lanyer, was again well-placed to have also written such works.

Could Thomas Deloney of the St Giles-without-Cripplegate parish, have allowed his name to be used by the powerful local Willoughby family, perhaps initially for the publications of the one-handed propagandist and secretary to Lord Willoughby, John Stubbe, who died in 1590, but then by

---

[45] Marsh, "Best-Selling Ballads and the Female Voice of Thomas Deloney", 150-152

[46] Deloney, *A True Discourse of the Most Happy Victories obtained by the French King*, EEBO image 10.

his "handmaid", Aemilia Bassano, who worried about abused women and "our defence"?

One more poem deserves mention. Deloney died in 1603, yet new editions of his *Strange Histories* continued to be published, in 1607 and 1612, with many additional poems by "Deloney", and continuing to show the predisposition to write from a woman's perspective. But one such poem in the 1607 edition (not the 1602 or 1612 editions) was not by Deloney. It is *A Mayde's Letter,* by A.C. It sets the scenario of separated lovers, with the maid declaring her love and commitment, essentially "till death do us part" as though written by a fiancée to her fiancé. The first and last (6th) stanzas of A.C.'s poem are shown below:

> Haste commendations and pass with speed
> And little writing of my Love:
> Spare not to speak for any dread
> For why, no man can me remove.
> Say this unto my Turtle-dove
> Although my body absent be,
> There is no man can me remove
> For in conceit I am with thee.
> ...
> When all these things become to pass
> Which I on spake, then, be assured
> You'll find these women brittle as glass,
> But not till then, if life be pure.
> Constant still I will endure,
> Whiles there's any life in my body;
> If I speak the words, I'll make them sure,
> And in conceit I'll end with thee.

This 1607 poem is full of idealism from a young betrothed woman with no hint of cynicism or disillusionment, in contrast to Deloney's own poems such as *A Gentlewoman's Complaint* or *The Woman's Answer*, in *Garland of Good Will* (1593). A.C. is apparently a young literate maid who wished to remain discreet and modest about her identity. Since her poem was in Deloney's anthology, she knew the feminist poet, Deloney, now deceased, or whoever she was.

This conundrum may be resolved if the "Deloney" publishing with a woman's perspective was Aemilia Lanyer, a poet known to be concerned about "our [women's] defence," and the fiancée, A.C., was Anne Clifford, Lanyer's pupil, who had just become engaged. Negotiations for Anne's marriage to Richard Sackville appear to have started as early as August,

1605,[47] and continued in the early summer of 1607.[48] After this long
engagement, in February, 1609, the nineteen years old Anne Clifford (1590-
1676) married Richard Sackville, 3rd Earl of Dorset as mentioned earlier.

In June of 1610, Anne Clifford, Countess of Dorset, performed in the
Tethys Festival masque, devised by her former tutor, Samuel Daniels, to
celebrate the investiture of Prince Henry as the Prince of Wales. This
masque involved several other dedicatees of Lanyer's *Salve Deus Rex
Judaeorum* (1611), in addition to Lady Anne. They included Anne Clifford's
close friend, Arabella Stuart, and Queen Anne, and her teenage daughter,
Princess Elizabeth. "Though your years be green", the fifteen-year-old
princess was compared to her godmother, Queen Elizabeth I, in the poem,
To the Lady Elizabeth's Grace (line 10). This celebratory moment may have
presented an opportunity to raise the female voice, particularly since the
chief censors of the press, John Whitgift and Richard Bancroft who had
sponsored Nashe's misogynistic rants, died in 1604 and 1610, respectively.

The persecution of John Stubbes in 1579 and Thomas Deloney in 1595/6
were demonstrations of the inherent dangers of publishing. Although
Princess Elizabeth Stuart's future husband was being actively considered
from Protestant and Catholic prospective partners alike, Lanyer offered no
advice, unlike the presumptuous recommendations made to the princess's
godmother, 32 years before in Stubbes' *Gaping Gulf* (1579). Yet her *Eve's
Apology* was potentially provocative. As it eventuated, it was the poem, *To
the Lady Arabella,* which had to be deleted from the presentation copy to
Prince Henry, because Arabella had married without the King's authority
and was sent to the Tower in March, 1611.[49]

Conclusion

In the 1593, there was a man, who identified as a woman, spoke for all
women and defended Eve. In 1611, there was a woman who spoke for all
women and defended Eve. In a parody of John Florio, this woman, Aemilia
Lanyer, claims that her book was "the first fruits of a woman's wit" in her
To the Lady Elizabeth's Grace (line 13). Can we believe her?

Aemilia Lanyer was *Philomel.* Philomel is the archetypal #MeToo
woman from Ovid's *Metamorphoses*; the abused, muted and trapped
woman who sent an SOS to her sister. Even after the pioneering example

---

[47] Williamson, *Lady Anne Clifford: Her Life Letters and Work*, 76.
[48] Malay, "Positioning Patronage: Lanyer's *Salve Deus Rex Judæorum* and the
Countess of Cumberland in Time and Place", 251-264.
[49] Ng, "Amelia Lanyer and the Politics of Praise", 436.

set by Aemilia Lanyer in 1611, women have understood the dangers of publishing and felt compelled to be duplicitous, preferring to adopt male names, – like George Elliot or George Sands, – or signed off as "Anon."[50] Are we being naïve to consider that the younger Aemilia Lanyer did not do much the same?

It is possible that Thomas Deloney was a compulsive emulator of the feminine persona, but this paper's proposal is that the assertive Aemilia Lanyer was publishing her poetry eighteen years or more before 1611, but using as an allonym, Thomas Deloney. A few assumptions must be made, just as assumptions must be made about the authorship attribution on title pages.

Marshall Grossman suggested that "presumably Aemilia Lanyer wrote more than the slim volume now extant, and it is doubtful that we have now enough of her poetry to sustain the kind of perpetual inquiry that creates and maintains canonicity".[51] If we here have her secret allonym, the Aemilia Lanyer canon can be increased considerably.

Bibliography

Barroll, Leeds. "Looking for Patrons". In *Aemilia Lanyer: Gender, Genre and the Canon,* edited by Marshall Grossman, 29-48. (Lexington: University Press of Kentucky, 1998).

Benson, Pamela Joseph. "To Play the Man: Aemilia Lanyer and the Acquisition of Patronage". In *Opening the Borders: Inclusivity in Early Modern Studies; Essays in Honor of James V. Mirollo*, edited by Peter C. Herman, 243-64. (Newark: Univ. of Delaware Press, 1999).

Bollard, Charlotte. 2011. *Italian Material Culture in the Tudor Court.* University of London: PhD Thesis.

Brown, Pamela. 2003. *Better a Shrew than a Sheep.* Ithaca: Cornell University Press.

Carlson, E.J. "Clerical Marriage and the English Reformation". *J. British Studies,* 31 (1992): 1-31.

Deloney, Thomas. 1589. *A True Discourse of the Most Happy Victories obtained by the French King.*

Florio, John. 1578. *His First Fruits.* Early English Books Online (or EEBO).

Grossman, Marshall, "Introduction". In *Aemilia Lanyer: Gender, Genre and the Canon,* edited by Marshall Grossman, 1-9. (Lexington: University Press of Kentucky, 1998).

---

[50] Virginia Woolf, *A Room of One's Own*, 50.
[51] Grossman, "Introduction", 8.

Hasler, P.W. (ed.), *History of Parliament: The House of Commons, 1558-1603*. (London: Boydell & Brewer, 1981), under "John Stubbe (c.1543-90)". Online https://www.historyofparliamentonline.org/volume/1558-1603/member/stubbe-john-1543-90 Hudson, John. 2014. *Shakespeare's Dark Lady: Amelia Bassano Lanier*. Stroud: Amberley Press.

Lake, Peter. "The Politics of Popularity". In *The Politics of the Public Sphere in Early Modern England,* edited by Peter Lake and Steven Pincus, 59-94. (Manchester: Manchester University Press, 2007).

Kempe, William, 1600. *Nine Days Wonder.*

Korp, Christopher. "Shoemakers, Clowns, and Saints: The Narrative Afterlife of Thomas Deloney." *UC Berkeley, Honors thesis*, 2015. Online https://www.academia.edu/28582241/SHOEMAKERS_CLOWNS_A ND_SAINTS_THE_NARRATIVE_AFTERLIFE_OF_THOMAS_DE LONEY

Lasocki, David. "Alvise Bassano". *Oxford Dictionary of National Biography.* Oxford: Oxford University Press, 2018.

Lewalski, Barbara. "Seizing Discourses and Reinventing Genres". In *Aemilia Lanyer: Gender, Genre and the Canon,* edited by Marshall Grossman, 49-59. (Lexington: University Press of Kentucky, 1998).

Lewalski, Barbara. 1993. *Writing Women of Jacobean England*. Cambridge, Mass.: Harvard University Press.

Lock, Anne. 1560. *The Sermons of John Calvin*, & *Meditations of a Penitent Sinner*. Early English Books Online.

Lock, Anne. 1590. *Of the Marks of the Children of God*. Early English Books Online.

McKerrow, Ronald (ed.). 1910. *The Works of Thomas Nashe,* Volume 5.

Malay, Jessica. "Positioning Patronage: Lanyer's *Salve Deus Rex Judæorum* and the Countess of Cumberland in Time and Place ". *The Seventeenth Century*, 28 (2013), 251-274.

Mann, F.O. (ed.), 1912. *Deloney's Works*. Oxford: Clarendon Press.

Marsh, Christopher. "Best Selling Ballads and the Female Voices of Thomas Deloney". *Huntington Library Quarterly*, 82 (2017): 127-154. Also online https://core.ac.uk/download/pdf/96665117.pdf .

Nashe, Thomas. 1589/90. *Anatomy of Absurdity*. Early English Books Online (or EEBO)

Nashe, Thomas. 1593. *Christ's Tear Over Jerusalem* (1593). Early English Books Online.

Nashe, Thomas. 1596. *Have With You To Saffron Walden*. Early English Books Online.

Ng, Su Fang. "Amelia Lanyer and the Politics of Praise". *English Literary History* 67.2 (2000): 433-451.

Raber, Karen. 2001. *Dramatic Difference: Gender, Class and Genre in the Early Modern Drama*. Newark: University Delaware Press.

Rowse, A.L. (ed.). 1979. *The Poems of Shakespeare's Dark Lady*. N.Y.: Clarkson N. Potter.

Williamson, George. 1922. *Lady Anne Clifford: Her Life Letters and Work*. London: Kendal, Titus Wilson & Son. Online https://archive.org/stream/cu31924027999014/cu31924027999014_djv u.txt .

Woods, Suzanne (ed.). 1993. *The Poems of Aemilia Lanyer: Salve Deus Rex Judaeorum*. N.Y.: Oxford University Press.

Woods, Suzanne. 1998. "Vocation and Authority: Born to Write". In *Aemilia Lanyer: Gender, Genre and the Canon,* edited by Marshall Grossman, 83-98. (Lexington: University Press of Kentucky, 1998).

Woods, Suzanne. 1999. *Lanyer: A Renaissance Woman Poet*. N.Y.: Oxford University Press.

Woods, Suzanne, "Anne Lock and Aemilia Lanyer: A Tradition of Protestant Women Speaking". In *Form and Reform in Renaissance England Essays in Honor of Barbara Kiefer Lewalski* edited by Amy Boesky and Mary Thomas Crane, 171-184 (London: Associated University Press, 2000).

Woolf, Virginia. 2000. *A Room of One's Own*, London: Penguin. First published 1928.

CHAPTER ELEVEN

EVIDENCE FOR AEMILIA LANYER'S PEN IN DELONEY'S NOVELLAS

MARK BRADBEER

The Queen at Tilbury (1588)

Thomas Deloney's broadsheet ballad, *The Royal Receiving of the Queen at Tilbury*, dating from the Armada crisis,[1] is unusual in several respects. In 1588, it is surprising that a mere "ballading silk-weaver"[2] could speak directly to the English people on the Queen's behalf. Deloney adopts the voice of the Queen, even to the extent of employing the royal "We" to promise the Queen's support for the Tilbury army (line 168), as shown, underlined, below (lines 161-170):

> And then bespake our noble Queen,
> My loving friends and countrymen:
> I hope this day the worst is seen,
> That in our wars ye shall sustain.
> But if our enemies do assail you,
> Never let your stomachs fail you.
> For in the midst of all your troop,
> <u>We</u> ourselves will be in place:
> To be your joy, your guide and comfort,
> Even before your enemies face.

As words of encouragement to her countrymen, Deloney verses rival the prose record of the Queen's speech.[3] Deloney's ballad is also unusual for its detailed and accurate account of the Queen's visit to the Tilbury army camp

---

[1] Francis Oscar Mann, *Deloney's Works* (Oxford: Clarendon Press, 1912), 474-8.
[2] Thomas Nashe, *Have With You To Saffron Walden* (1596), EEBO image 51.
[3] A.N. Wilson, *The Elizabethans* (London: Arrow Books, 2012). 257. The chaplain, Dr Leonel Sharp, recorded this speech at Tilbury.

during an impending invasion by the Spanish Armada. For example, how would Deloney know that the Queen stayed "at Master Riche's for that night" (line 93) of Monday, 8th of August 1588 before her official review of the army on the Tuesday? Edward Riche (d.1599) was a minor local Justice of the shire.

Despite many Elizabethan broadsheet ballads being now lost, this ballad survived, possibly suggesting that it had a large print run, was widely-distributed and had many new reprints. It is likely that authorities were familiar with this ballad. It was registered. Most curiously, the ballad was registered one day after the Queen's speech at Tilbury.[4]

Deloney's biographer, Francis Mann, envisaged Deloney registering his ballad "as a modern newspaper reporter hurries his exclusive news into print".[5] Was Deloney an on-the-spot reporter at Tilbury, or a desk-bound London journalist translating a report into verse? If we imagine Deloney to be one of the thousands in the army at Tilbury, his going absent-without-leave at this moment of crisis, to visit London printers and the Stationers' Register would have been severely punished. If Deloney had contacts in the Queen's entourage, the problem is not much better resolved, as bad weather delayed their return to London to late Wednesday, 10th August. Any messenger within the entourage had to liaise with our supposed desk-bound journalist for immediate versification of the Tilbury report, then arrange for a publisher to go the Stationers' Register near St Paul's churchyard to register his ballad before closing hours the same day.

Authorship by the simple, independent silk-weaver, Thomas Deloney, is increasingly problematic. It looks like this ballad had some official sanction. James McDermott referred to Deloney's Armada ballads as "effective propaganda, and the speed with which these works appeared indicates that they were little else."[6] Let us look at two potential official sources. Both the Earl of Leicester and Lord Hunsdon could have provided an informed and confidential report by express post on the 9th of August, or even prior notice about the Queen's Tilbury event.[7]

When, on the 27th of July, the Earl of Leicester suggested to the Queen that she visit the army camp, he wrote, "ye shall comfort not only these

---

[4] Francis Oscar Mann, *Deloney's Works* (Oxford: Clarendon Press, 1912), xxxvii.

[5] Francis Oscar Mann, *Deloney's Works* (Oxford: Clarendon Press, 1912), xxxvii.

[6] James McDermott, *England and the Spanish Armada*, (New Haven and London: Yale University Press, 2005), 279. See also John McAleer, "Ballads on the Spanish Armada", *Texas Studies of Literature and Language*, 4 (1963), 606.

[7] James McDermott, *England and the Spanish Armada*, (New Haven and London: Yale University Press, 2005), 279.

thousands [at Tilbury] but many more than shall hear it" [i.e. her speech].[8] From the outset, the Queen's Tilbury visit was planned as a morale-boosting exercise, not just for those at Tilbury, but for the nation. The nation was at war. And in this time of deep anxiety, this ballad had to be delivered immediately across the nation, to be sung by the literate and the illiterate alike. The Elizabethan ballad broadsheet was, indeed, the newspaper of the times – a bit more sophisticated than the network of burning beacons and tolling bells which had initially alerted all England of the Armada's approach at the end of July. An ally of Leicester was John Stubbes, secretary to Lord Willoughby and known government propagandist.[9] Stubbes had assisted Leicester in scuppering the Queen's marriage plans with the Duke of Anjou by publishing his pamphlet, *The Gaping Gulf* (1579), nine years before. Based on Tilbury information from the Earl of Leicester, this secretary at Willoughby House may have composed the ballad. But if Aemilia Bassano had not yet become mistress to Lord Hunsdon by 1588,[10] the Willoughby-mentored poet may still have been employed at Willoughby House and lent him some assistance.

Lord Hunsdon (1526-1596) was also at Tilbury. He accompanied the Queen as Captain of the Queen's bodyguard. Also known as Henry Carey, he was cousin of the Queen, a member of the Privy Council and the Lord Chamberlain. As Lord Chamberlain, he was also in charge of Royal entertainments. With him as the Tilbury source for the ballad, he could have commissioned this *The Royal Receiving of the Queen at Tilbury* from one of his employees, a number of whom were of the Bassano family of musicians. Some scholars have suggested that Aemilia Bassano had become Lord Hunsdon's paramour by 1588.[11] With the possibility that Lord Hunsdon was the Tilbury source, he simply commissioned his mistress/poet to convert his report into ballad form for prompt registration and publication.

---

[8] Marion Colthorpe, *The Elizabethan Court Day by Day*, for 1588, Folgerpedia Online 2017.

[9] Lake, Peter. "The politics of popularity and the public sphere: the 'monarchical republic' of Elizabeth I defends itself". In *The Politics of the Public Sphere in Early Modern England*, ed. Peter Lake and Steven Pincus. (Manchester: Manchester University Press, 2007). 74, 76, 77.

[10] Susanne Woods, *Lanyer: A Renaissance Woman Poet* (N.Y. and Oxford: Oxford University Press, 1999), 16.

[11] John Hudson, *Shakespeare's Dark Lady* (Stroud: Amberley Press, 2014), 30; and A.L. Rowse, *The Poems of Shakespeare's Dark Lady* (N.Y.: Clarkson N. Potter, 1979), 14; and David Bevington, "Rowse's Dark Lady", In *Aemilia Lanyer,* ed. Marshall Grossman (Lexington: University Press of Kentucky, 1998), 19, respectively.

In contrast to Aemilia Bassano, Thomas Deloney has no known links with these two noblemen.

Peerless Deloney?

Ironically, eight years after Deloney's Tilbury broadsheet, his ballad, *On the Want of Corn* (1596),[12] upset authorities because it engaged in "certain vain and presumptuous matters, bringing in the Queen, speaking with her People dialogue-wise in very fond and undecent sort."[13] Many Elizabethans seem to have forgotten Deloney's contribution to the war effort in 1588 when he also brought "in the Queen speaking to her people" in *The Royal Receiving of the Queen at Tilbury*. Those who might have defended Deloney, such as the Earl of Leicester (1532-88), John Stubbes (c.1543-90) and Lord Hunsdon (1526-96) were dead. As a result of the ballad, *On the Want of Corn* (1596), Deloney became a wanted man.

In 1600, Shakespeare's clown, William Kemp, seems to have come to Deloney's rescue, by prematurely announced the death of Thomas Deloney as follows:

> My notable Shakerags! ... the great ballad-maker, T.D., alias Thomas Deloney, chronicler of the memorable lives of *The Six Yeomen of the West*, *Jack of Newbury*, *The Gentle Craft*,[14] and such like honest men – omitted by Stow, Holinshed, Grafton, Hall, Froissart, and the rest of those well-deserving writers – but I was given since to understand your late general, Thomas, died poorly (as ye all must do) and was honestly buried, which is much to be doubted of some of you. The quest of inquiry finding him by death acquited of the Inditement.

Contrary to Kemp, the researcher, Alan Nelson, found Deloney's burial record to be dated 1603.[15] But by virtue of Kemp's acquittal of the ballad-maker "by death", Deloney may have found some peace in his last three years of life.

Thus, "the great ballad-maker, T. D. alias Thomas Deloney" has left behind a litany of anomalies. Did he know the Queen or didn't he - either in 1588 or 1596? Was he alive or dead after 1600? Scholars also puzzle over

---

[12] Thomas Deloney's 1596 ballad, *On the Want of Corn,* did not survived its total censorship.
[13] Francis Oscar Mann, *Deloney's Works* (Oxford: Clarendon Press, 1912), ix.
[14] These books are also known as *Thomas of Reading* (1597), *The Pleasant History of John Winchcomb* (1597), and *The Gentle Craft, Part 1* (1597) and *Part 2* (1598).
[15] Christopher Korp, "Shoemakers, Clowns, and Saints: The Narrative Afterlife of Thomas Deloney", 5.

the question: "Who would Deloney have considered his peer, and who would have considered Deloney their peer?".[16] He employed the royal "We" when writing morale-boosting ballads. He could translate Latin. He "yarked-up" ballads to be sung in ale-houses,[17] yet penned moralistic ballads like *Thunderbolt against Swearers* and *Repent, England, Repent.*[18] It has also been observed that the ballads of Deloney" identified with women, wrote from a feminist perspective, and expressed sympathy for abused courtesans and husband-killers, praise Aemilia Bassano Lanyer's mentors in the Willoughby family and encourage the poetic skills of Lanyer's pupil, Anne Clifford.[19] Consequently, Aemilia Bassano Lanyer has been proposed to have used "T.D. alias Thomas Deloney", as her allonym.

One would therefore predict that there is similar evidence for Lanyer in Deloney's novellas, mentioned above by Kemp. Superficially, this appears incorrect as *The Six Yeomen of the West* and *Jack of Newbury*, are ostensibly about Deloney's main occupation, which was weaving. Yet *The Gentle Craft, Part One* and *Part Two* are ostensibly about the shoe-making industry, and no-one is proposing that the poet was a shoemaker. Perhaps the presumption that the silk-weaver Deloney published what he wrote, and wrote what he experienced, is wrong.

Examples from two Deloney novellas will be examined to show that they are more easily explained as issuing from Lanyer's pen, rather than Deloney's.

The Gentle Craft, Part Two (1598)

Deloney's book, called *The Gentle Craft, Part Two* (1598), is set during the reign of Henry VIII, and it contains the ballad, *The Song of The Winning of Bullen,*[20] beginning (lines 1-6):

In the month of October
Our King he would to Dover
By leave of Father and the Son

---

[16] John Carpenter, "Placing Deloney*", J. Narrative Theory*, 36 (2006): 125-162, partic. 153.

[17] Robert Greene, *Defence of Cony Catching*, 1592, EEBO image 4.

[18] Thomas Nashe, *Have With You to Saffron Walden*, 1596, EEBO image 51.

[19] Mark Bradbeer, "Are Lanyer's *Eve's Apology* (1611) and Deloney's *In Praise of Women* (1593) from the Same Poet's Pen?". In *Stratified Nature: Women's Writing, Past Present and Future*, ed. Marie Hendry (Newcastle-upon-Tyne: Cambridge Scholar, **2022?**)

[20] Francis Oscar Mann, *Deloney's Works* (Oxford: Clarendon Press, 1912). 168-9.

A great army of men
Well-appointed there was then,
Before our noble King to come.

The army proceeds to the French city of Bullen/Boulogne-sur-Mer. The song then metamorphoses into a siege of a woman, not the French city, with lines like:

Our King hath sent to prove you (line 25)
Because that he doth love you. (line 26)
Fair Bullen is a famous Maiden town (line 33)
She is lady of most high renown (line 36)

The penultimate verse is (lines 49-54):

This Maiden town that lately
Did show herself so stately
In seeking favour, many tears she shed:
Upon her knees then fell she down,
Saying, O King of high renown,
Save now my life, and take my maiden-head.

Henry VIII's October campaign on the French port of Bullen occurred in 1523.[21] This was well before Henry VIII's courtship of Anne Bullen/Boleyn and close to the time of Mary Bullen's concubinage to Henry VIII.[22] Mary was Anne Boleyn's sister, and Henry Carey's mother. There is also the suspicion that Henry VIII was Henry Carey's biological father.

The 70-years old Henry Carey, Lord Hunsdon, died on the 23rd of July, 1596. Although *The Gentle Craft, Part Two* was published in 1598, it is not known when this ballad was composed. This song appears to be designed to appeal to Lord Hunsdon's fondness for his much-abused mother, his proximity to royalty, as well his liking of military history. It was a personal poem, which probably was only publishable after his death. Deloney's authorship again is problematic. It is proposed here that this poem was authored when Aemilia Bassano herself was Hunsdon's young paramour. She would have had the knowledge, skill and insights to write this work.

---

[21] See www.british-history.ac.uk/report.aspx?compid=91129, whereas the 1544 campaign was from July to September.

[22] David Loades, *The Boleyns*, (Stroud, UK: Amberley, 2011). 51. This suggests that she was the King's mistress from 1523, lasting 3 to 5 years. Reports (www.british-history.ac.uk/report.aspx?compid=91129) show the father of Mary and Anne, Sir Thomas Bullen, receiving grants from the King in September, 1523. Als

Jack of Newbury (1597)

Deloney's book, *Jack of Newbury*, is also set during the reign of Henry VIII and is about the "famous and worthy clothier of England", John Winchcomb. The biographer, Francis Mann notes that Deloney "shows a detailed knowledge of Newbury, its surroundings, and the county families of Elizabethan Berkshire."[23] Lanyer's beautiful poem about the Berkshire village of Cookham – *Description of Cookeham* – supports her familiarity with Berkshire.

In chapter 2 of *Jack of Newbury,* Jack's wife is out late and he locks her out of the house. After much pleading from his wife, Jack lets her into the house but she tricks him and locks him out of the house instead. This gendered episode is sourced from *The Decameron* by Boccaccio.[24] There was no English translation of this story.in 1597. Deloney's biographer, Francis Mann, identified this conundrum, struggled to explain it, and attributed Deloney's inspiration for the story to a generalized "floating mass of popular Elizabethan literature".[25]

Mann was unable to identify the source for the dozen or more notable people in Jack's portrait gallery in chapter 5 of *Jack of Newbury*. These are various men of poor origins who lived to become rich and powerful, like the Portugese King Viriat, the Sicilian King Agathocles, the Athenian-born Persian general, Iphicrates, and many Roman Emperors and Popes. These days we can identify Deloney's source to be the untranslated Latin work published in Basel, *Exemplorum Hoc Est, Dictorum Factorumque Memorabilium* (1567) by Baptista Campofulgoso (sometimes written Battista Fregosol). These characters are less likely to be from a "floating mass of popular Elizabethan literature". It appears that the author could access and read relatively uncommon Latin and Italian literature.

Chapter 4 is all about King Henry VIII's jester, Will Summers, who barely rates a mention in the rest of *Jack of Newbury,* and serves no role in the overall story. His presence may have more topical relevance to the 1590s. The misogynist, Thomas Nashe, derided women in his *Anatomy of Absurdity* (1589), and challenged them to "stop my mouth", even though there was no level playing field for women to publish.[26] Indeed, nothing resembling equality existed, and, besides, Nashe's patron was the chief press censor. Nashe returned to his railing against women in his *Christ's*

---

[23] Francis Oscar Mann, *Deloney's Works* (Oxford: Clarendon Press, 1912), 507.
[24] Giovanni Boccaccio, *The Decameron* (London: Penguin Books, 1995), 501-5.
[25] Francis Oscar Mann, *Deloney's Works* (Oxford: Clarendon Press, 1912), 508.
[26] Thomas Nashe, *Anatomy of Absurdity* (1589), EEBO image 5.

Tears Over Jerusalem (1593).[27] Responses to these two Nashe attacks may be in Deloney's feminist *In Praise of Women* (1593) and Lanyer's *Eve's Apology in Defence of Eve* (2011), respectively.[28]

In his *Pierce's Supererogation* (1593), Harvey lauded an unnamed female poet and chastised Nashe, identifying him as the metaphorical reincarnation of the clown, Will Summers, from the court of Henry VIII.[29] Harvey may have seen or heard about Nashe's play, *Summers Last Will and Testament*, written in 1592 and first performed the same year at Croydon palace before his patron, the chief censor, John Whitgift, Archbishop of Canterbury. In this play, Will Summers' ghost is a surrogate for Nashe.[30]

Chapter 4 of *Jack of Newbury,* begins with the following interesting episode featuring Will Summers:

> How the maidens served Will Summers for his sauciness… They bound him hands and feet, and set him upright against a post, tying him thereto… And because he let his tongue run at random, they set a fair gag in his mouth… Then one of them got a couple of dog's droppings and put them in a bag, laid them to soak in a basin of water, while the rest turned down the collar of his jerkin … then came the other maid with a basin and the water in the same, and with the perfume of the pudding bag, slapt him about the face and lips, till he looked like a tawny Moore.

This humiliating assault was supposedly for Summers' attempt at stealing kisses, yet it appears to be an overreaction. Its gendered nature and more particularly the silencing of Will Summers' tongue with a gag in his mouth, is more explicable as an intertextual response to Thomas Nashe's challenge to women "to stop my mouth."

---

[27] Thomas Nashe, *Christ's Tears Over Jerusalem* (1593), EEBO images 75, 77, 81-84.

[28] Mark Bradbeer. "Are Lanyer's *Eve's Apology* (1611) and Deloney's *In Praise of Women* (1593) from the Same Poet's Pen?". In *Stratified Nature: Women's Writing, Past Present and Future*, ed. Marie Hendry (Newcastle-upon-Tyne: Cambridge Scholar, **2022?**)

[29] Gabriel Harvey, *Pierce's Supererogation* (1815), 150.

[30] Sheri Geller, "Commentary as Cover-Up: Criticizing Illiberal Patronage in Thomas Nashe's *Summer's Last Will and Testament*", *English Literary Renaissance*, 25 (1995): 148-178, esp. 173. Also, Reid Barbour, *Biography of Thomas Nashe*, Poetry Foundation. Online
http://www.poetryfoundation.org/bio/thomas-nashe , *accessed 18/8/2021.*

Conclusion

Like previous research on T.D.'s ballads, the Lanyer theory for T.D. authorship gives a simple explanation for the apparent multiplicity of masks worn by T.D. as novelist. The theory explains the creative drivers for the works, in contrast to that of the man employed full-time as silk-weaver. Lanyer was an outcast on the margins in so many ways – as Hunsdon's secret paramour, as a commoner, but most particularly because of her sex. Prior to, and after, her publishing of *Salve Deus Rex Judaeorum* (1611), women's freedom in the press to defend their own sex continued to be censored by institutional and non-institutional means.

An example is an unnamed gentlewoman writer who contended with Nashe is described by Gabriel Harvey. He called her "my patroness, or rather my championess in this quarrel", but "I dare not particularise her description … without her licence or permission that standeth upon masculine, not feminine terms."[31] Publishing required standing "upon masculine terms," otherwise misogynists like Nashe would make derisive, lewd sexual allusions to them. Despite Harvey being non-specific about his gentlewoman poet, Nashe, found ways to attack her in his *Have With You to Saffron-Walden* (1596). Nashe developed a dialogue between male characters who, first, denying her existence, say that she is Harvey's invention and that authorship can hardly "proceed from a woman."[32] Then Nashe's characters liken her to a whore and a harlot, and threaten to "strip her to her smock."[33]

There is no consensus about the identity of Harvey's specific woman but recent research suggests that Harvey's unnamed gentlewoman writer in 1593 was Aemilia Bassano Lanyer,[34] eighteen years before publishing her *Salve Deus Rex Judaeorum* (1611). As his *Have With You to Saffron-Walden* (1596) was published a few months after Lord Hunsdon died, Nashe had little need to be careful if this female writer was Aemilia Lanyer.[35]

---

[31] Harvey, Gabriel, *Pierce's Supererogation* (originally Wolfe, 1593, published London: Longman, Hurst, Rees, Orme and Brown, 1815), 10, 208. See Internet Archive online
https://archive.org/details/piercessupererog00harvrich/page/n3/mode/2up .
[32] Thomas Nashe, 1596. *Have With You To Saffron-Walden.* EEBO image 67.
[33] Thomas Nashe, 1596. *Have With You To Saffron-Walden.* EEBO image 68.
[34] Mark Bradbeer, *Aemilia Lanyer as Shakespeare's Co-Author* (Oxford: Routledge, 2022), 89, 90, 118-9, 135-6.
[35] Thomas Nashe, 1596. *Have With You to Saffron-Walden.* EEBO image 47 refers to "the late deceased Countess of Derby", who died on the 28th September, 1596. This publication was therefore after Lord Hunsdon's death on the 24th July, 1596

Nashe's "quarrel" with Harvey, hid an unspoken *querelle des femmes*; that is, if quarrel includes sexualized verbal abuse. But there was always the chance of according a woman writer too much significance by merely abusing her. It elevated her to the status of an equal, and the right of reply. It was better to deny her existence as author altogether, then there was no quarrel to have.

Prior to her example in 1611, when she published in her own name, articulate women like Aemilia Lanyer had no option but be anonymous, pseudonymous or allonymous, to defend themselves, and their sex, from bullies of establishment mores like Nashe.

Bibliography

Barbour, Reid, *Biography of Thomas Nashe*, Poetry Foundation. Online http://www.poetryfoundation.org/bio/thomas-nashe , *accessed 18/8/2021.*

David Bevington, "Rowse's Dark Lady", In *Aemilia Lanyer* edited by Marshall Grossman, 10-28. (Lexington: University Press of Kentucky, 1998),

Boccaccio, Giovanni. 1995. *The Decameron.* London: Penguin Books.

Bradbeer, Mark, 2022. *Aemilia Lanyer as Shakespeare's Co-Author.* Oxford and N.Y.: Routledge.

Bradbeer, Mark, "Are Lanyer's *Eve's Apology* (1611) and Deloney's *In Praise of Women* (1593) from the Same Poet's Pen?". In *Stratified Nature: Women's Writing, Past Present and Future*, edited by Marie Hendry (Newcastle-upon-Tyne: Cambridge Scholars Press)

Carpenter, John. "Placing Deloney*"*. *J. Narrative Theory*, 36 (2006): 125-162.

Colthorpe, Marion. "The Elizabethan Court Day by Day". Accessed August 25th, 2021. Folgerpedia online: https://folgerpedia.folger.edu/The_Elizabethan_Court_Day_by_Day#A uthor.27s_Introduction .

Geller, Sheri. "Commentary as Cover-Up: Criticizing Illiberal Patronage in Thomas Nashe's *Summer's Last Will and Testament*". *English Literary Renaissance*, 25 (1995): 148-178.

Greene, Robert. 1592. *Defence of Cony Catching.* Early English Books Online.

Harvey, Gabriel, *Pierce's Supererogation* (originally Wolfe, 1593, published London: Longman, Hurst, Rees, Orme and Brown, 1815). See Internet Archive online https://archive.org/details/piercessupererog00harvrich/page/n3/mode/2 up .

Harvey, Gabriel. 1593. *A New Letter of Notable Contents*. In appendix of *Pierce's Supererogation* by Gabriel Harvey (originally Wolfe, 1593, published London: Longman, Hurst, Rees, Orme and Brown, 1815). See Internet Archive online https://archive.org/details/piercessupererog00harvrich/page/n3/mode/2 up .

Hudson, John. 2014. *Shakespeare's Dark Lady*. Stroud: Amberley Press.

Lake, Peter. "The politics of popularity and the public sphere: the 'monarchical republic' of Elizabeth I defends itself". In *The Politics of the Public Sphere in Early Modern England*, edited by Peter Lake and Steven Pincus. (Manchester: Manchester University Press, 2007).

Loades, D.2011. *The Boleyns*. Stroud, UK: Amberley.

Mann, Francis Oscar. 1912. *Deloney's Works*. Oxford: Clarendon Press.

McAleer, John. "Ballads on the Spanish Armada". *Texas Studies of Literature and Language*, 4 (1963): 602-612.

McDermott, James. 2005. *England and the Spanish Armada*. New Haven and London: Yale University Press.

Nashe, Thomas. 1593. *Christ's Tears Over Jerusalem*. Early English Books Online.

Nashe, Thomas. 1596. *Have With You to Saffron Walden*. Early English Books Online.

Nashe, Thomas. "Summer's Last Will and Testament". In *Thomas Nashe: The Unfortunate Traveller and Other Works* edited by J.B. Steane (London: Penguin, 1985).

Rowse, A.L. 1979. *The Poems of Shakespeare's Dark Lady*. N.Y.: Clarkson N. Potter.

Wilson, A. N. 2012. *The Elizabethans*. London: Arrow Books.

Woods, Susanne. 1999. *Lanyer: A Renaissance Woman Poet*. N.Y. and Oxford: Oxford University Press.

CONTRIBUTORS

Rashmi Attri has worked at Jamia Millia Islamia, New Delhi as faculty for the department of English for 25 years. Her areas of interest include Indian English Writings, Indian subaltern women's narratives, Afro- American literature, Ecological humanities, and ELT. She has published around 20 papers in reputed national and international journals dealing with different areas of her interests. She teaches Modern British and Elizabethan Drama, English for Business, Postcolonial Fiction, Theories and Methods of Second Language Teaching, Teaching Language through Literature, Indian Aesthetics, etc. at Graduate and Postgraduate levels.

Hatice Bay, Cappadocia University, studied English Literature at METU, Turkey and graduated with a PhD in American Literature from the University of Hamburg. Her research interests include contemporary American literature, cli-fi, city literature, literature of immigration and road narratives.

Amanda Bell is an award-winning Irish poet and writer. Her books include *Revolution* (haiku chapbook, wildflower poetry press, 2022), *Riptide* (poetry collection, Doire Press, 2021), *the loneliness of the sasquatch* (a transcreation from the Irish of Gabriel Rosenstock, Alba Publishing, 2018), *First the Feathers* (poetry collection, Doire Press, 2017), *The Lost Library Book* (creative non-fiction for children, The Onslaught Press, 2016), and *Undercurrents* (a psychogeography of Irish rivers, Alba Publishing, 2016).

Mark Bradbeer lives in Australia. He is a former research nurse with a publication record in the biomedical sciences. His current interests are in Early Modern authorship issues, and he has published on Aemilia Lanyer as Shakespeare's co-author, the 1593 Dutch Church Libel involving playwright, Kit Marlowe, and Shakespeare's History plays.

Jim Coby is Assistant Professor of English at Indiana University Kokomo. His work has appeared in numerous scholarly journals and his co-edited collection *Boom! Splat!: Comics and Violence* is forthcoming from the University Press of Mississippi.

Jeff Darwin (cover artist) is an instructor and program manager of graphic design at State College of Florida. He has both a Master of Arts from Florida State University in International Affairs and Master of Arts in Art from Northwestern State University of Louisiana.

Teresa Fitzpatrick is a post-graduate researcher at the Manchester Centre for Gothic Studies and an Associate Lecturer in English at Manchester Metropolitan University. Her doctoral thesis, *Killer Plants and Gothic Gardeners* developed a material ecofeminist Gothic framework to explore the intersection of gender and cultivated nature in speculative fiction from the late nineteenth to the twenty-first century. She has written reviews on ecoGothic/ecohorror for several journals, presented her research at numerous conferences, and contributed chapters on nature and gender, ecoGothic, and eco-posthumans to various edited collections.

Marie Hendry is Associate Professor of Language and Literature at State College of Florida, with a PhD in literature from the University of Louisiana at Lafayette. Her current publications include "Motherhood as Ecological Metaphor in Nnedi Okorafor's *Lagoon*" in *Alluvium* and *Agency, Loneliness, and the Female Protagonist in the Victorian Novel* through Cambridge Scholars Publishing.

Dr. Laura Holder is originally from Southeast New Mexico. She received her doctorate in English from University of Louisiana at Lafayette, with a focus on Early American literature & pop culture. She currently teaches English & Humanities at Odessa College in Odessa, Texas.

Dr. Shubhanku Kochar is currently working as an Assistant Professor at University School of Humanities and Social Sciences at Guru Gobind Singh Indraprastha University, Delhi. He has been teaching since 2012. His areas of interest include African and African Diasporic Literature along with Ecological literary criticism. He is also a member of MELOW the society for Multi-ethnic Literatures of the World and IACLALS known as Indian Association of Commonwealth Literatures and Language studies. He has written a novel titled Everything Will Be Alright, and his other publications include Treatment of Violence: A Reading of Toni Morrison's Selected Fiction and An Eco-critical Reading of Alice Walker's Selected Works, both published by Lambert Academic Publishers of Germany. He has also published nineteen research papers in national and international journals. He has also presented various research papers at national and international conferences. He has contributed book chapters for publishers like Lexington

Press, an imprint of Rowman and Littlefield, Vernon Press, Maria Grzegorzewska University Press, Routledge, and Cambridge Scholars Publishing. He has published his latest book Environmental Post-Colonialism: A Literary Response 2021 with Lexington Press, an imprint of Rowman and Littlefield, which can be accessed at the following link, https://rowman.com/ISBN/9781793634566/Environmental-Postcolonialism-A-Literary-Response

Arush Pande is a 1st year graduate student in English at Princeton University. He received his BA in English from Ashoka University, near New Delhi, and completed his MA from the Department of English at Lehigh University in Bethlehem, Pennsylvania. Arush wants to study the various tropes and idioms that characterize the literature of the Anthropocene in the 20th and 21st century. He is particularly interested in narratives of environmental justice, especially those that emerge from the Global South. When he is not sobbing over a book in a quiet corner, you can find him waving to strangers' dogs, or endorsing Bollywood 'masala' films to anyone who cares to listen.

Wendy Whelan-Stewart is an associate professor of English at McNeese State University. She teaches American literature and has published articles on twentieth-century North American women writers. She is currently researching American women writers' depictions of breastfeeding mothers.